T0331049

Companies That Mimic Life

Leaders of the Emerging Corporate Renaissance

Companies
that Mimic Life

Leaders of the Emerging Corporate Renaissance

Joseph H. Bragdon

Routledge
Taylor & Francis Group

LONDON AND NEW YORK

First published 2016 by Greenleaf Publishing Limited

Published 2017 by Routledge
2 Park Square, Milton Park, Abingdon, Oxon OX14 4RN
711 Third Avenue, New York, NY 10017, USA

Routledge is an imprint of the Taylor & Francis Group, an informa business

Copyright © 2016 Taylor & Francis

Cover by Sadie Gornall-Jones

British Library Cataloguing in Publication Data:
A catalogue record for this book is available from the British Library.

ISBN-13: 978-1-78353-543-9 [hbk]
ISBN-13: 978-1-78353-542-2 [pbk]

Contents

Figures and tables

Figures

Tables

Foreword

Giles Hutchins

We are in the midst of a metamorphic period unlike anything the world has seen since the Late Middle Ages. There is a transformative change in form of the human institutions now emerging as we awaken to the realities of climate change and the destruction of ecosystems we rely on for our survival. As the organization specialist Peter Drucker insightfully said, "In times of turmoil, the danger lies not in the turmoil but in facing it with yesterday's logic."

Nowhere is this metamorphic change more evident than in the way businesses are being organized and managed. The ideal of "organization-as-machine," which was dominant for hundreds of years into the late 20th century, is now giving way to an ideal of "organization-as-living-system." As a conceptual shift, it affects all aspects of our enterprising futures: from how we perceive the world about us, to the ways we think and manage and the evolution of our technology down to the ways we manufacture our cars. The implications are huge. Corporations that seize the breadth and depth of this shift in thinking will be tomorrow's success stories; those that don't will be yesterday's news.

To not just survive but thrive in this new norm of increasing volatility, our leaders must deepen their personal and organizational capacity to sense into the emerging field of future possibilities while unlocking the creative potential of the organization. It requires a widening of our perceptual horizon from old habitual patterns of management and control to a more conscious sense of what it means to create and deliver value in an increasingly interconnected, digitized fast-moving world.

Whether it's via the disciplines of quantum physics, psychology, ecology, neurobiology, organizational development, or sociology, it is now dawning on us that life is not simply a mechanistic construct of push–pull factors and selfish genes, where separate organisms compete with each other in the struggle for survival. Rather, our modern scientific lens now allows us to recognize what ancient wisdom traditions the world over have long perceived: that life is an inter-relational network of inter-being, where everything is in dynamic relation with its environment, continuously communicating and collaborating within an ocean of being.

In this perceptual field, the "self" is not the "separate self" of individualism but the "differentiating self" immersed within a rich milieu of relations. Ditto for the organization, which provides specific value within its niche as a living system intimately entwined within its wider social and ecological ecosystem. It is the diversity and reciprocity of these relations that provides for a living system's resilience and, in turn, the resilience of the wider ecosystem. As Leonardo Da Vinci succinctly put it, "Learn how to see. Realize everything connects with everything else."

Our worldview of life is presently transforming from one of separateness, competition, and self-agency to one of interwoven relationality, where a dynamic order amid unceasing transformation prevails due to natural patterns, feedback loops, behavioral qualities, interdependences, and adaptations. The quicker our leaders, managers, and change agents embrace this worldview, the better for organizations and wider humanity. I, for one, am encouraged by how this living-systems view of life is beginning to permeate our corridors of power. *Companies that Mimic Life* is a vital contribution to this necessary revolution.

Increasingly, as our organizational context requires us to become ever more emergent, innovative, and adaptive, so leadership must become more about empowering, empathizing, encouraging interconnections, innovation, learning, local attunement, reciprocating partnerships, and an active network of feedback. As such, the aim of leaders becomes more focused on nurturing conditions where the organizational living system can unlock its creative potential, learn, and flourish in a purposeful and coherent way, so that it can create and deliver value while being mindful of the wellbeing of all the people it serves and the wider fabric of life it relates with. This is not some utopian dream; it is the fundamental purpose of any wholesome economic activity, and the fundamental purpose of our humanity. More and more business people the world over are recognizing this and transforming their ways of operating and organizing in the process.

The insights we need for today's challenges lie all around and with us if we so choose to look. By opening ourselves more to how life really is (beyond the habituations, acculturations, and control-based frames of yesterday's logic) we allow a deeper and richer perspective to form within us. We bring forth organizations that enhance our humanity rather than stifle and constrain our creativity, that empower us to become more purposeful and authentic rather that enslaving us in ways that demean and undermine our humanity. And the good news is: this all makes perfect business sense.

Companies that Mimic Life goes right to the heart of the matter by providing much-needed strategic insight supported by hard financial performance data and detailed case studies of seven corporations embracing the logic of living systems. Experienced and respected investment adviser Jay Bragdon examines what defines their success: their abilities to learn from living systems, which awaken a deeper human consciousness that galvanizes their organizations toward more purposeful, flourishing futures in harmony with life. After all, this is the only viable way ahead for us. I cannot recommend this timely and important work highly enough for those actively engaged in the future of business.

Giles Hutchins is the cofounder of Biomimicry for Creative Innovation and author of *Future Fit*, and other books

Dedication and acknowledgment

This book is dedicated to the late Donella (Dana) Meadows, who understood that transformative change—regenerating the Earth's over-stressed biosphere and reforming broken social systems—requires a different mode of thinking from the ones that caused these problems in the first place. As lead author of the 1972 classic, *Limits to Growth*,[1] she long ago urged us to adopt a new mode of thinking focused on systemic health rather than continuing to exploit and degrade ecological and social systems in our bottom-line-first pursuit of growth.

To achieve this paradigmatic transformation, Dana noted in her celebrated essay, "Leverage Points," that there are "places within a complex system (a corporation, an economy, a living body, a city, an ecosystem) where a small shift in one thing can produce big changes

---

1   Donella H. Meadows, Dennis L. Meadows, Jørgen Randers, & William W. Behrens III (1972). *The Limits to Growth* (New York, NY: Universe). Retrieved from http://www.donellameadows.org/wp-content/userfiles/Limits-to-Growth-digital-scan-version.pdf.

in everything."[2] That is the underlying premise of this book.

By looking on companies as living systems rather than mechanical ones (a legacy of the Industrial Revolution), we can achieve that shift. Dana and I often talked about this before her untimely death and it is the reason she invited me to serve on the board of the Sustainability Institute, which she founded. What we both sought to develop was a new narrative, replete with real-world examples that would help to turn the tide.

Among those who have helped me develop this book, I most of all want to recognize the patience, presence, and encouragement of my wife, Jeanne, who has been my thinking partner for the last 16 years: from the very start of my research and writing through to the final editing of its text. As a deep ecologist and accomplished writer, her insights and advice have been priceless.

As my manuscript approached completion, I have also been grateful for advice and feedback from Alan AtKisson, Katherine Collins, Hal Hamilton, Steen Hildebrandt, Giles Hutchins, Ted Kellogg, Shyla Nelson, Riichiro Oda, Frank Peabody, David Peart, and Darcy Winslow—all of whom have critiqued or otherwise contributed to my manuscript.

Looking further back in time, I am indebted to the late Forrester Clark, General Partner of the formerly top-rated investment research firm, H.C. Wainwright & Company. In the early 1970s he allowed me to initiate a new branch of research focused on the relationship between corporate stewardship and profitability—an addendum to the firm's mainstream offers. The evolution of that research, which took me deeply into systems thinking, has been the most gratifying element of my professional life.

JHB

2   Donella Meadows (1999). Leverage points: places to intervene in a system. Retrieved from http://donellameadows.org/archives/leverage-points-places-to-intervene-in-a-system/.

Introduction

> We are at that very point in time when a 400-year-old age is dying and another is struggling to be born—a shifting of culture, science, society, and institutions enormously larger than the world has ever experienced. Ahead, the possibility of the regeneration of individuality, liberty, community, and ethics such as the world has never known, and a harmony with nature, one another, and with the divine intelligence such as the world has never dreamed.
>
> Dee Ward Hock, founder of Visa[1]

Industrial capitalism is broken. The signs, which transcend national ideologies, are everywhere. Climate change. Ecological overshoot. Financial exhaustion. Fraying social safety nets. Corporate fraud. Government deceit. Civic unrest. Terrorism. War.

---

1   M. Mitchell Waldrop (1996, October 31). The trillion-dollar vision of Dee Hock. *Fast Company*. Retrieved from http://www.fastcompany.com/27333/trillion-dollar-vision-dee-hock.

Yet, with the world approaching unimaginable economic and social chaos, a transformative new system is emerging. This book tells how that transformation is taking root in the corporate world—the last place many of us would look for solutions.

This is not to say the years ahead will be easy. They will be difficult. Many—if not most—economic, ecological, and social problems will become worse before they get better. But there is hope. And Dee Hock, the visionary founder of Visa, frames it accurately.

In these pages, I intend to show why Hock's uplifting vision of the future is credible. My thesis is embedded in the stories of seven exceptional companies. Their shared secret is a new mental model of the firm that is the virtual opposite of industrial capitalism.

It works like this: instead of modeling themselves on the assumed efficiency of machines—a thought process that emerged during the industrial age—these firms model themselves on living systems. Understanding that everything of value ultimately arises from life, they place a higher value on *living* assets (people and Nature) than they do on *nonliving* capital assets. The energy they invest in stewarding those assets—a practice we call "living asset stewardship" (LAS)—is transformative. Instead of exploiting people and Nature, which creates systemic resistance, they nurture both, which creates flow and harmony.

When you step back and think of this approach, it makes sense. Companies are inherently living systems—communities of people with shared goals—living and working at the intersection of biosphere and society. And here is the rub: within this web of life there resides enormous intelligence, much of which remains untapped.

Life-mimicking companies tap into this intelligence in two key ways:

1. Through mimicking natural processes in the ways they produce goods and services (via industrial ecology)

2. By awakening the spiritual intelligence of employees, which resides in the interconnected neurology of their hearts, brains, and guts

We will return to these themes many times in our narrative. For now, suffice it to say that spiritual intelligence is our highest intelligence because it guides our reasoning ability (IQ) and emotional intelligence by investing them with meaning and purpose. Through the modern sciences of cognition we are still learning how these processes work.

Progressive companies—particularly those featured in this book—are on the leading edge of that discovery process because they recognize adaptive learning as essential to both competitive excellence and survival.

This brings us to the urgent *raison d'être* of companies that mimic life. Given the ecological and social disintegration of the world economy under the system of industrial capitalism, we must learn to live and work more harmoniously with the rest of life. And learn fast.

Systems thinker Peter Senge calls this awakening of human consciousness "a necessary revolution." And it is. Companies at the forefront of this revolution, by connecting to the immense resources of the human spirit, will survive and thrive through the challenges we now face. Those in denial will certainly fail.

The crux of the matter is this: the lenses through which we view the world (our mental models of reality) ultimately determine our outcomes. Companies that mimic life see the world as it actually is: a self-regulating, complex, adaptive system whose defining property is life—not a mechanical system that works by a fixed set of laws.

The incontrovertible fact is: no other planet in our solar system has evolved such a diversity of ecosystems. From the bacteria that regulate our climate to the intricate web of plants and animals that comprise Nature, to our very human selves whose advanced brains have conceived sophisticated markets and institutions of learning, the Earth is unique. As companies that mimic life have learned, the path to success in such a world is to integrate with and learn from life, rather than separating ourselves from it as omnipotent conquerors and controllers. Call it unconventional, if you will, but it works.

Companies that mimic machines don't get this. By ignoring the reality that they are part of life and that they utterly depend on life for the value they create, they short-circuit their capacities to learn and adapt and consign themselves to a lose–lose cycle of compounding errors.

The Global LAMP Index®

In the early 1990s, respected authors began to advance the idea of economies as ecosystems and companies as living entities within those systems. Seminal books of this movement included Michael Rothschild's *Bionomics: Economy as Ecosystem* and Peter Senge's *Fifth Discipline*—both published in 1990. This conceptual paradigm evolved at MIT, where both men did their doctoral studies, through the pioneering work of Jay Forrester, the father of systems thinking.

The underlying premises of these books awakened me to new insights. While my earlier training in economics and securities analysis had prepared me to see the world in an empirical (linear) way—with emphasis on discrete numbers, such as gross domestic product (GDP), revenues, and corporate earnings—this new mode of thinking enabled me to see systems as a whole and the importance of diverse nonlinear feedbacks in determining outcomes.

In hindsight, I was mentally ready for this shift in thinking. Since the early 1970s, I had observed that companies with progressive cultures were outperforming those with more traditional bottom-line-first cultures, yet I didn't have a cohesive theory to explain why.

To explore this new ground, I helped to organize, and cochaired, the first national symposium on "Corporate Responsibility in Investments" at the Harvard Business School in April 1972. Although a step forward, the ideas that emerged from this meeting left too many questions unanswered. As I look back on it, the insights we sought were not to be found in reductionist number crunching or end-of-the-pipe solutions, but in looking upstream to question the fundamental premises of business as usual.

To shorten a long story, as I became immersed in systems thinking a light went on. If companies were living ecosystems, their primary assets had to be living as well. Although implicit in the behavior of many progressive companies, nobody at the time had made a clear distinction between living assets and nonliving capital assets. Once made, however, LAS seemed a high-leverage thing to do.

To test that idea, in 1995 I created a learning lab of companies that were then stewardship leaders. Called the Global Living Asset Management Performance (LAMP) Index®, this lab has since become a continuing source of insight: a means of tracking the evolution of LAS best practices in a group of committed stewardship leaders.

Starting with a small cohort of companies I knew well from prior years of research, I gradually expanded the index to 60 companies (double the size of the Dow Jones Industrial Average)—large enough to be statistically significant, but small enough that I could keep up with current developments in each. By selecting "best of breed" LAS companies within a broadly representative group of industries/sectors, I was able to deepen my insight into the synergies of life-mimicking cultures while achieving the high degree of comparability that I sought.[2]

To maintain the lab's integrity, its composition has been remarkably stable. Of the original 60 companies, there have been only six name changes since 1995, the notional start date of the Index: four due to mergers and acquisitions and two due to original selection errors on my part. By minimizing the bias of hindsight, this stability enables us to make credible comparisons of investment returns on the LAMP60 relative to benchmark indices.

Table 0.1 indicates the operating advantages of LAS relative to conventional management practices. Looking at multiyear periods between 1996 and 2015, we see the LAMP60 outperformed by wide margins three commonly used global equity benchmarks: the Morgan Stanley Capital International (MSCI) World Index; the Financial Times Stock Exchange (FTSE) World Index; and the Standard & Poor's (S&P) Global 100 Index.

Good as Global LAMP Index® returns have been, however, the learning lab conveys a larger message: that the deeper companies go into LAS, the more profitable they become.

To test that proposition, I separated from the original LAMP60 seven companies that model LAS best practices. Called the "Focus Group," these cover a range of industries from steel and capital goods to consumer durables (apparel), nondurables (household products), pharmaceuticals, and banking. Although not perfectly comparable to the LAMP60, due to its overweight in manufacturing

---

2   The investment consultancy Northfield Information Services (http://www.northinfo.com) has run multiple tests on the comparability of the LAMP60 to a variety of global benchmark indices (2006, 2007, 2014, 2015). These indicated r^2 results in the range of 0.90–0.95, which suggests a high degree of correlation.

TABLE 0.1   Shareholder returns 1996–2015
Cumulative compound growth

Years	Global LAMP Index®			Global comparator indices		
	Focus Group (eq. wt.)	LAMP60 (eq. wt.)	LAMP60 (cap. wt.)	FTSE (cap. wt.)	MSCI (cap. wt.)	S&P 100 (cap. wt.)
20	1618.76	1023.85	482.33	275.09	251.59	361.78
15	781.70	240.89	133.63	108.89	94.80	82.92
10	288.72	112.31	82.35	77.41	71.00	101.68
5	84.04	46.18	46.15	46.57	47.54	80.23
3	43.72	34.46	30.87	34.00	31.92	50.52
1	6.81	-5.70	-2.71	2.58	-1.84	2.63

and zero weight in technology, the Focus Group nevertheless makes a powerful case for pursuing best practices.

In fact one of the key lessons derived from the Focus Group is how **the advantages of LAS best practices are magnified in mature industries, where older theories of management predominate.** By enabling progressive companies to out-think competitors, they generate factor efficiencies and market share gains that yield extraordinary shareholder returns.

Consider the case of Nucor. Operating in the deeply cyclical, lay-off-prone steel industry, it has been profitable in all but one of the past 50 years (1965–2015) with no lay-offs due to lack of work. During this time, which included seven U.S. recessions, declining U.S. steel output, and widespread bankruptcies among U.S. steelmakers, Nucor's shares appreciated in value more than 400-fold.

Fascinating as Nucor's story is—and we shall return to it shortly—we should not assume that our LAS leaders have a locked-in competitive advantage. In fact, their advantages are likely to diminish over time as other companies copy, and improve on, their practices. This is natural. Good ideas spread and eventually drive out bad or less effective ones.

In LAS, as with product and process innovation, the only way to stay ahead is to continuously push LAS best practices, to stay on the leading edge of the learning curve. The Focus Group is remarkable because its seven companies have done this better than most of the LAMP60 cohort.

The advantages of best practices are especially evident during and immediately following economic recessions, where speed of learning and adaptation convey strategic advantages. During the five-year period that began with the recession of 2000–2002, the Focus Group returned 109%—more than double the LAMP60, which gained 49%—while global benchmarks lost 13% on average. Again, looking at the five-year period starting with the market crash of 2008 and ensuing recession, the Focus Group returned 52%—more than triple the LAMP60, which gained 14%—while global benchmarks lost 4% on average.

The operating leverage of LAS

The operating leverage of LAS, as just suggested, resides in speed of learning and adaptation. These skills, in turn, rely on a heightened corporate consciousness. Because consciousness is a unique property of life, the more lifelike companies become, the more conscious they become.

So what are these critical lifelike qualities? There are six. And they are present in all life from single-cell organisms to large ecosystems. These include:

1. **Decentralized, self-organizing networked structures,** whose component parts serve the health of the whole

(such as the human nerve system and the cognitive architecture of our brains)

2. **Regenerative life strategies** that increase opportunities for survival, reproduction, and improving cultural DNA

3. **Frugal instincts** that seek to optimize use of resources

4. **Openness to feedback** that enables adaptive learning

5. **Symbiotic behaviors** that link individual wellbeing to the health of the larger systems in which they exist (biosphere, society)

6. **Consciousness** of capabilities, interdependences, and limits

The sixth is an emergent quality that grows as the other five attributes become more developed, and is important because it guides the capacities of companies to make intelligent decisions.

To show how these life-mimicking attributes work in practice, our first seven chapters describe how the seven Focus Group companies use them to leverage their cognitive skills, which is the source of their extraordinary ecological, social, and financial results. While many of these qualities have been explored in academic and business studies, this book is the first to present them as a coherent whole.

In Chapter 1, we begin with a holistic overview of LAS through the experience of Unilever: a producer of household goods, rated as one of the world's most ethical and sustainable companies. Our story highlights the company's Sustainable Living Plan, which aims to radically lower its global ecological footprint while raising living standards in developing countries, where it sources many of its raw materials. As one of the world's most sought-after employers, Unilever attracts an extraordinary depth of young talent. The energy so generated accelerates profit growth. Between 2000 and 2015, the value of its shares appreciated more than 200%—roughly five times more than global benchmark indices and 1.3 times more than its primary competitor, Procter & Gamble.

In Chapter 2, we discover how Nucor reinvented the global steel industry by giving frontline employees the creative freedom to **self-organize** and **network**. By simply harvesting the knowledge of men and women doing the work, it quickly became the innovation, profit, and green leader of its industry with no research and development (R&D) department. Between 2000 and 2015 Nucor's shares grew by more than 450%—nine times more than global benchmark indices—while the once-giant US Steel lost shareholder value.

In Chapter 3, we learn how the United Technologies Corporation, a manufacturer of capital goods, developed a capacity for **self-regeneration** by serving the personal and professional growth of employees. Its employee scholarship program, initiated in 1996, enables all employees, regardless of rank, to pursue the degree of their choice, up to PhD, at company expense. Degrees in art and philosophy are as valid as those in math and business. Instead of being a drain on corporate finances, this investment in building network capacity has helped United Technologies become a global leader in green engineering. Between 2000 and 2015 its stock grew by more than 250%—five times more than global benchmark indices—in a period when the shares of engineering giant General Electric lost value.

In Chapter 4, we see how Novo Nordisk became the profit leader of the global pharmaceutical industry by inspiring employees to think in a resource-conserving, holistic context. Because of its commitment to responsible **frugality**, Novo has remained virtually debt-free, giving it the liberty to deepen its explorations into industrial ecology and to broaden its learning culture. Between 2000 and 2015

Novo's share price appreciated more than 20-fold, while those of Merck, Pfizer, and Lilly (Novo's main competitor) all lost value.

In Chapter 5, we learn how Henkel preserves a **culture of openness** through free and transparent information sharing toward achieving its goal of "factor three" efficiencies (defined as producing three times as much from a given set of resources). To accentuate open, honest communication, top executives serve as "personally liable partners." Between 2000 and 2015, Henkel's shares appreciated 450%—approximately nine times more than global benchmark indices.

In Chapter 6, we learn how Nike uses innovation to pursue its **symbiotic** goal of effecting "environmental, labor and social change." By freely sharing its knowledge on open-source platforms, it has accelerated constructive change in the apparel industry. Since 2007, *Fast Company* magazine has six times rated Nike among the world's "top 50" innovative companies (#1 in 2013, #17 in 2014). Between 2000 and 2015, its shares appreciated more than 1,200%—about 25 times more than global benchmark indices.

In Chapter 7, we learn how Westpac Banking raised its corporate **consciousness** by creating a culture "in which everyone is able to think clearly and creatively, to act ethically, and to air any issues or concerns absolutely without fear." Long regarded as the world's "most sustainable bank," under CEO Gail Kelly it was named in 2014 the world's most sustainable company. Between 2000 and 2015, Westpac's shares appreciated more than 270%—roughly four times more than those of JPMorgan Chase—and its Moody's credit rating (Aa2) was higher as well.

When the six attributes of living systems are combined—as they are in all seven Focus Group companies—the thinking capacities of a firm are greatly magnified. The first level of magnification, as we shall see from the case studies in Chapters 1–7, arises from engaging the minds of all employees rather than just those of top executives. The second, and arguably the more powerful, comes from the **inspired thinking** of employees who seek to make the world a better place.

The reinforcing cycle of LAS

Looking more deeply into the cultures of life-mimicking companies, we encounter a meta-leverage point: one that catalyzes and accelerates their speed of learning and adaptation. It is the human heart.

When people work with their hearts as well as their minds, they engage the powerful heart–brain neurology that is the source of their highest (spiritual) intelligence. As mentioned earlier, this spiritual intelligence guides their emotional intelligence and IQ by giving both a sense of direction and meaning.

FIGURE O.I The reinforcing cycle of LAS and profit

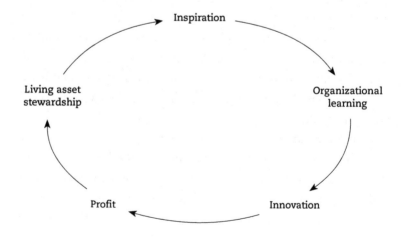

The way this meta-leverage works can be visually summarized as a reinforcing cycle. Like all durable theories, it is conceptually simple as shown in Figure 0.1.

Reading clockwise from the left, we see how the cycle operates. LAS inspires employee learning and collegial collaboration. The resulting organizational learning accelerates innovation. Innovation, in turn, catalyzes profit. The loop becomes reinforcing as profit returns to strengthen LAS.

The power of this cycle is **organic** and will be a continuing theme as we move from chapter to chapter. Companies that use it effectively achieve higher returns on equity in spite of using less **mechanistic** debt leverage than their industry peers. As a result, the average and median credit ratings of the LAMP60 are in the A3 range (Moody's) and those in the Focus Group are in the A3/A2 range— all solidly investment grade. By contrast, the average and median ratings of all the world's rated corporations are on the threshold of junk and below.

An emerging renaissance

By placing a higher value on living assets than on nonliving capital assets, LAS has reversed the strategic priorities of industrial capitalism. As discussed in Chapters 8 and 9, this awakening constitutes a powerful reinvention of capitalism and, more hopefully, a reintegration of humanity into the biospheric web of life.

Like the European Renaissance and Reformation of the 14th–17th centuries, during which people moved away from long-standing theocratic (God-centered) beliefs toward a more humanistic (anthropocentric) worldview—indeed, coming to believe in ourselves as masters of Nature—today we are gravitating away from that self-centered mind-set toward a more holistic (ecocentric) worldview.

This emerging shift in human perception, like that of the earlier Renaissance, occurs at a time when disruptive anomalies call into question old beliefs while scientific insights open the mind to new possibilities.

The disruptive anomaly of the 14th century was the bubonic plague, which killed a third of Europe's population. Today it is the threat of climate change and ecological overshoot, which threaten all life.

The scientific insights of that earlier period involved humanity's capacity to reason and to imagine a real world that was separate from Church dogma. Today's sciences of cognition, quantum theory, ecology, and system dynamics take us deeper into our own potential and the interdependence of all life.

Living asset stewardship as learning journey

LAS has come a long way in the past few decades as an evolving practice of corporate management. Nevertheless, the companies featured in this book will be the first to admit that they still have a lot to learn.

Living and working within the limits of the Earth's biological resources is a moving target. Nothing in Nature or human society stands still. Beyond that, we have to remediate a glut of damages we have done to the biospheric web of life. Consequently, the need for adaptive learning is both continuous and urgent.

Given the urgency of this challenge, I have chosen to focus on these seven LAS exemplars, rather than the entire LAMP60, because they are best qualified to show us a way forward. By highlighting their harmonic, symbiotic processes at work, I hope to encourage further research into the field.

To further advance such research, the appendices to this book share for the first time my full list of LAMP60 companies. Although this list would be different if I started it fresh today, my early selections have held up pretty well—both as stewards and as investments.

While some readers may dispute my use of energy and mining companies in the LAMP60, my goal was to assess "best of breed" within prominent global industries/sectors. Otherwise, comparisons with the selected benchmark indices would have been meaningless.

As a final note, had I decided each year to replace a few underachievers, as socially screened investment indices often do, the LAMP60 might have yielded better performance. But that is not the point of this learning lab. One of my core objectives was to see how the original list of LAS pioneers evolved. Would they rest on their laurels and become complacent? How would they address emerging new challenges? Had I made continuous substitutions I would have missed many of those nuances.

Looking back in time, many of the longest-lived LAMP companies have reinvented themselves many times because of their openness to new ideas. Evolution is not a smooth path. It moves in fits and starts.

That is why we must look on LAS as a learning journey, a continuous process of cultural evolution. As Nike is fond of saying, there is no finish line.

1

Changing paradigms

> Paradigms are the sources of systems. They are the assumptions that govern our behavior.
>
> Donella Meadows[1]

> The vision we set ourselves is to double the business and outperform market growth, whilst at the same time reducing our overall environmental impact.
>
> Paul Polman, CEO, Unilever[2]

The world of business is in the midst of a major paradigm shift from the long-standing machine model of the firm to an emerging

---

1   Donella Meadows (1999). *Leverage Points: Places to Intervene in a System*. Hartland, VT: Sustainability Institute. Retrieved from http://donellameadows.org/wp-content/userfiles/Leverage_Points.pdf.

2   Paul Polman (2010). Speech to Unilever's Annual General Meeting. Retrieved from https://www.unilever.com/Images/paul-polman-agm-speech-2010_tcm244-418634_en.pdf.

one that mimics living systems. Having briefly described the new paradigm in the Introduction, this chapter tells the story of Unilever—an original member of the Global LAMP Index® and a leader in the new paradigm's development.

Unilever is the world's second-largest manufacturer of food and household products with annual revenues exceeding $70 billion. It is comprised of two separate British and Dutch companies— Unilever Ltd. (London) and Unilever NV (Rotterdam)—operating under a shared board of directors. It is also parent to hundreds of quasi-independent operating companies with products sold in more than 190 countries. With so many moving parts, one wonders how Unilever can operate coherently as an organic whole; much less, how it has emerged to become a global sustainability and profit leader.

The key is to think of Unilever as a large ecosystem: an organic network comprising millions of individuals (species)—employees, suppliers, customers, and other stakeholders—who collectively use their expertise and exchanges of value to grow the health and abundance of the whole system. Thinking of the company as such presents a radically different mental model of the firm than the more prevalent hierarchical one we find at most companies. And, as we shall see, it works brilliantly.

Consider the facts. In the 16 years since the turn of the millennium (2000–15), Unilever's shares returned roughly five times the S&P 500 Index and 1.3 times its largest direct competitor, Procter & Gamble. In January 2016, Corporate Knights listed it for the 12th consecutive year as one of the world's 100 most sustainable companies. In 2015, it was a sector leader in the global Dow Jones Sustainability Index for the 16th consecutive year—one of a rare few companies to sweep both indices since they were conceived. In May 2015, for the fifth straight year, the GlobeScan survey—which spans experts from business, government, nongovernmental organization (NGOs), and academia across 87 countries—rated Unilever by a wide margin as the number one corporate leader in sustainability.

Wonderful as these credentials are, Unilever is the subject of this chapter for one other compelling reason. In 2009, the company committed to a deeply life-affirming goal: to halve the environmental footprint of its products while doubling its sales and helping to improve the living standards of more than a billion people in emerging markets, where it sources its raw materials. This strategy, called "the Compass," is the heart of the Unilever Sustainable Living Plan and it has powerfully accelerated the reinforcing cycle of living asset stewardship (LAS), organizational learning, innovation and profit discussed in the Introduction (Figure 0.1).

The importance of such idealistic visionary goals cannot be overstated—especially for companies, such as Unilever, which have radically decentralized structures and localized decision-making. Employees connect more effectively when they are inspired by their work than when they are ordered to meet statistical (profit) goals handed down from a remote hierarchy. They are more responsive when treated as respected partners instead of mechanistic factors of production; and they become more engaged when they believe their opinions and insights matter. These advantages give firms organized around life-affirming goals an inner cohesiveness that eludes those organized around profit alone.

At Unilever, the evolution of such cultural qualities reflects a growing awareness that the firm itself is a living system—a community of people—working at the intersection of the larger living systems of biosphere and society on which all commerce depends. From this perspective, the health of the firm is symbiotically linked to the health of these larger systems and to the spiritual wellbeing of employees, who want their lives and work to matter.

When CEO Paul Polman introduced the Sustainable Living Plan, few companies were thinking beyond incremental reductions in their ecological footprints. He nevertheless took this leap of faith, sensing that Unilever's lifelike qualities endowed it with a unique capacity to achieve the plan's ambitious goals. And he was right. Since the Sustainable Living Plan was introduced, Unilever has become one of the world's most popular employers, a status—affirmed by both Glassdoor and LinkedIn—that enables it to attract an extraordinary depth of young talent.

To investors who questioned or disagreed with Unilever's new strategy, Polman famously responded: "Don't put your money in our company."[3] It was an audacious challenge to money managers to begin thinking beyond the short term and it sent a message to employees that he had confidence in their ability to meet the new goals.

Early focus on living assets

Nearly two decades before Polman introduced the Sustainable Living Plan, the firm decided to double down on its historic steward-ship model—a legacy of William Lever's 19th-century ideal of making the world a better place—and began to move toward a more symbiotic stakeholder focus. A key part of this mental shift was an implicit recognition that living assets (people and Nature) are the source of capital assets, which meant Unilever's future resided in how well it stewarded those assets.

---

3   Josie Ensor (2011, July 5). Unilever's Polman hits out at City's short-term culture. *The Telegraph*. Retrieved from http://www.telegraph.co.uk/finance/newsbysector/retailandconsumer/8617022/Unilevers-Polman-hits-out-at-Citys-short-term-culture.html.

This change of focus coincided with a new emphasis on Asian markets, which in the early 1990s were growing nearly twice as fast as more mature ones in the U.S.A. and Europe. Reflecting on the ethnic diversity of these markets and the need to understand their tastes, then Chairman and CEO, Floris Maljers decided to reorganize Unilever in a way that would benefit from everybody's creativity and experience within a structure that shared a common vision and understanding of corporate strategy. Accordingly, he began to give business units more localized autonomy. Described as "streamlining," the idea was to push decision-making out to the front lines where knowledge of local conditions and needs was most keen.

One of Maljers' greatest insights was to understand the importance of natural resources in these (and other) markets, where populations and consumer demands were beginning to stress local ecosystems. Consequently, he committed Unilever to three fundamental principles:

1. Sustainable agriculture

2. Sustainable fishing

3. Clean water

As Unilever shifted its focus to new emerging markets, it also brought indigenous people into the management of its business units, which were then spread over 75 countries. To these new employees, Unilever's culture of stewardship and respect was salutary and they responded by becoming committed partners in the company's success. As a result, Unilever's productivity and profits in Asian markets surged. In keeping with the reinforcing cycle of LAS, this reinforced the morale of employees and their commitment to Unilever's goals.

Raising the ante on living asset stewardship

In the two decades since Maljers moved Unilever toward a culture of LAS, humanity's global ecological footprint and climate change shifted from being marginal corporate concerns to vitally important risk issues. In fact, the year before the Sustainable Living Plan was launched, global markets crashed: an event caused by the convergences of ecological overshoot, financial overreach, and related economic stresses.

Discerning the linkages between these stresses, and the growing threats they posed to global commerce, Polman raised the ante on Unilever's culture of stewardship. By directly addressing the systemic causes of the malaise, his Sustainable Living Plan set a new standard in the emerging paradigm of companies that mimic life.

To Polman, as with other forward-thinking corporate leaders, the most worrisome aspect of this cycle of ecological decline and financial overreach was how the two elements reinforced each other and accelerated their deleterious effects. Since the late 1970s, when humanity's ecological footprint began to overtake the Earth's biological carrying capacity, there had been a parallel rise of borrowing in the world's industrial economies. Although possibly unrelated at the start, as time progressed, this debt became increasingly linked to ecological overstep as the costs of pollution, ecosystem collapse, climate change, and social stress built up in world economies.

The resulting rise of global debt/GDP ratios was later compounded by the explosive growth of financial derivatives. These bets on the future direction of asset prices quickly became a device for gaming stressed markets and credit conditions. In 2008, when global financial markets crashed, the notional amount of derivatives outstanding in world markets reached an astonishing $684 trillion—roughly ten times world GDP.

To Polman, the convergence of collapsing ecosystems with the explosion of debt and derivatives was taking the world economy in precisely the wrong direction. What he saw was an increasingly dangerous bubble based on the false notion that nonliving capital assets (via financial engineering) could compensate for the ongoing degradation of the Earth's biological carrying capacity.

Although such behavior may have seemed rational and necessary to those living *inside* the bubble, those who saw it in a more systemic context recognized that the world of commerce was in ethical crisis and in dire need of change.

The crisis of 2008, which I've always called a crisis of ethics more than anything else, has made a lot of people think differently about the way our society needs to function. Not in the sense of questioning capitalism *per se*—I'm a capitalist at heart as well—but in questioning the way that we achieve this.

Paul Polman, CEO, Unilever[4]

The renowned physicist and historian, Thomas Kuhn, who coined the term "paradigm shift," had a name for unanticipated negative feedback effects, such as those that caused the 2008 crash. He called them "anomalies." As these accumulate and reveal previously unforeseen systemic weaknesses, they compel people to seek new insights and solutions.

---

4   Paul Polman (2012, May). Interview: Unilever's CEO on making responsible business work. *Harvard Business Review*. Retrieved from https://hbr.org/2012/05/unilevers-ceo-on-making-respon.

The remarkable attribute of Unilever and other Global LAMP Index® companies is that they saw the anomalies of industrial capitalism far ahead of their peers and began to experiment with new approaches that put life at the center of their thinking rather than on the periphery. In doing so, they discovered better ways to understand and relate to the living world of society and Nature that is the ultimate source of their profit.

This book is all about such harmonic strategies. It presents LAMP companies as living, adaptive learning organizations seeking to thrive in a fast-changing ecological, social, and business environment. As indicated in the Introduction, their approach to managing in this milieu is to operate with full-spectrum consciousness (described in Chapter 7)—an awareness they attain by becoming more competent at mimicking life (described in Chapters 2–6).

Given the acceleration of global ecological overshoot, climate change, debt/GDP ratios, and related challenges, companies need such awareness as never before. If they don't continually learn and adapt as these conditions change, no matter how good they once were, they will be vulnerable.

Paul Polman clearly understood this. He also knew there is a limit to what top corporate leaders can do to effect change on the front lines where the company does most of its business. If Unilever was to be effective, it would have to address the whole system, not just part of it. That is why a critical part of its Sustainable Living Plan was to engage people in Unilever's hundreds of local business units in cocreating new solutions.

The rationale behind this policy was simple. The only way to engage the whole living system in which Unilever operated was to engage the eyes, ears, and senses of the whole organization. That meant stepping away from traditional command-and-control policies and creating a radically decentralized network of self-organizing local cells, much like the organs of the human body.

Dee Hock, the visionary founder of Visa, called this a "chaordic" organization: a term he used to describe the way "autocatalytic, nonlinear, complex, adaptive systems" create order on the edge of chaos. To imagine how it works, envision a forest ecosystem.[5] There is no hierarchy here, only a web of interconnected food chains in which organisms, from bacteria up, self-organize in seemingly chaotic ways to produce a well-ordered system whose strengths exceed the sum of its individual parts.

The leverage in biomimicry

Human organizations work best when they operate on the chaordic principles found in Nature. As mentioned in the Introduction, this leverage is realized in two ways:

1. By engaging the minds of all employees rather than just those of top executives (which broadens corporate vision)

2. By inspiring employees with visionary goals of making the world a better place (which deepens corporate vision)

While both forms of leverage are important, the second type is the more powerful because it engages the spiritual intelligence of employees, which invests their IQ and emotional intelligence with a sense of direction and meaning. This is the type of intelligence that drives the reinforcing cycle of LAS (shown in Figure 0.1).

While there is no precise way to measure spiritual intelligence, companies can do it in a general way by regularly assessing employee engagement. According to a 2014 report by the consultancy Aon

---

5   Dee Hock (n.d.). The art of chaordic leadership. Retrieved from http://www.meadowlark.co/the_art_of_chaordic_leadership_hock.pdf.

Hewitt, companies that achieve 76% or greater on employee engagement surveys outperform the average company on revenue growth (by 6%), operating margin (4%), and total shareholder return (6%).[6]

By this standard, Unilever's Sustainable Living Plan has achieved a good deal of success. In the five calendar years since it was introduced, the company's engagement scores grew from the low 70s (2010) to 77% in 2014. Reflecting this, the company experienced steady increases in operating margins (from 12.6% in 2010 to 14.5% in 2015) and returns on equity (from 27.9% to 34.7%) while increasing market share.

As further evidence of Unilever's operating leverage, it launched in March 2014 a first-of-its-kind £250 million ($415 million) green bond offering. Described as "transformational" by underwriter Morgan Stanley, bond proceeds were intended to replace old factories with new ones that would halve the previous amounts of waste, water usage, and greenhouse gas emissions. The bond's indenture also included an innovative feedback reporting structure that enabled full traceability of funds so investors would know that proceeds were being spent properly.

The offering itself was a wonderful example of inspired intelligence. It was unique and transformational with clear ecological goals and metrics. Investors loved it. The five-year offering, which offered a 2% fixed coupon, was oversubscribed many times over, reflecting investor confidence in Unilever's vision and ability to execute.

As we will see throughout this book, these linkages between LAS and economic performance—measured in terms of corporate

---

6   Aon Hewitt (2014). *2014 Trends in Global Employee Engagement*, p. 9. Retrieved from http://www.aon.com/attachments/human-capital-consulting/2014-trends-in-global-employee-engagement-report.pdf.

returns on equity, shareholder returns, access to credit, and longevity—are grounded in sound principles that anyone can understand.

In the following section we explore why this is so by comparing the emerging life-centered model of the firm to the more traditional model that predominates today.

The two models in brief

An easy way to grasp these differences is to visualize companies as a metaphoric iceberg, where the top 10%, which we see above water, represents measurable results, such as earnings, and where the bottom (foundational) 90% represents the core beliefs, corporate cultures, and behaviors that generate those results.

The traditional model, as shown in Figure 1.1, was founded on a common assumption of the early Industrial Revolution: that natural resources are limitless while capital, the means of leveraging those resources, is scarce. Although empirically true at the time, this idea led early industrialists to a mistaken belief that capital took precedence over life.

This capital-centered mind-set evolved from the 17th-century mathematics of René Descartes and the scientific methods of Sir Francis Bacon, which became amplified in the 18th century by the physics of Sir Isaac Newton. One of the core ideas that emerged from their works is that humanity has a "right" to dominion over Nature. It even supported subsequent beliefs that we could mechanize our own behavior—a theory held by the behaviorist school of psychology.

Taken to the extreme, this capital-centered mind-set advanced beliefs that people and Nature could be harmed in the interest of

FIGURE 1.1   Traditional model of the firm

Results	Measurable effects on GDP, profit, society, biosphere	→ Systemic failure
Behaviors	Maximize profit Ignore external costs	→ Systemic stress
Structures	Hierarchical, linear Reductive, mechanistic	→ Dehumanizing → Disconnected
Vision and values	Machine-like efficiency, capital begets capital The quickest way to higher living standards	→ Devalues life → Shortsighted
Beliefs	Limitless natural resources, perpetual growth Technology leverages labor and nature Capital assets have more value than people and nature	→ Diminishes life

creating a better life for society as a whole. During the 19th century this became embedded in "the greatest happiness principle" of the utilitarian philosopher Jeremy Bentham and the unrestrained capitalist theory of Jean Batiste Say.

These assumptions, beliefs, and mind-sets underlie the vision and values that drive the traditional model of the firm and these, in turn, determine its structures and behaviors. Consequently, we find embedded in that model, and in classical economics, a vision of the company as a money-making machine, where capital begets capital in a reinforcing cycle of limitless growth.

Embedded in that vision are reductionist values that venerate machine-like efficiency, where employees are seen as replaceable factors of production and where life that exists apart from the machine (biosphere and society) is treated as "externalities."

As suggested in Figure 1.1, this narrow, capital-centered perspective feeds back in harmful ways because it devalues and degrades the very sources of the firm's future wellbeing.

The structures that emanate from such visions and values support management hierarchies that are more focused on ends (the bottom line) than on the means to those ends (employees, natural resources, biospheric conditions). Reinforced by "scientific management" theory and behaviorist psychology, such disconnects unavoidably lead to behaviors that are dehumanizing and stressful to the larger corporate ecosystem.

That stress feeds back to many of the adverse conditions we see today, such as disruptive climate change, collapsing fisheries, depleting fresh water supplies, rising public health costs, widespread social unrest, and compounding debt/GDP ratios.

Within traditionally managed firms, such stresses naturally call into question management judgment and ethics. When employees sense that this is part of a larger picture of executive voracity and corporate empire building, staff morale, and engagement decline. That decline, in turn, erodes productivity, customer service and ultimately profit.

This negative cycle of poor employee engagement and declining results correlates with the declining life expectancies of traditionally managed companies. As the deleterious effects of unsustainable debt, ecological damage, and employee alienation weigh on profits, the average life-span of companies listed in the S&P 500 Index has fallen from 61 years in 1958, to 25 years in 1980, to 18 years today.[7]

---

7   Innosight (2012). *Creative Destruction Whips Through North America*, p. 2. Retrieved from http://www.innosight.com/innovation-resources/strategy-innovation/upload/creative-destruction-whips-through-corporate-america_final2015.pdf.

FIGURE 1.2   Organic model of the firm

Results	Measurable effects on GDP, profit, society, biosphere	→ Prosperity
Behaviors	Steward living assets Harmonize with web-of-life Profit devoted to higher ends	→ Systemic health
Structures	Servant leadership Life-mimicking companies Holistic systems thinking	→ Creative → Synergistic
Vision and values	Bio-centric, ethical, imaginative	→ Inspiring
Beliefs	Natural and social limits to growth Harmony with living systems is key to prosperity People and nature more important than capital assets	→ Life-affirming

While defenders of the old system say these shorter average life-spans reflect the increasing pace of technology, the truth lies elsewhere because the average and median ages of life-mimicking companies in the Global LAMP Index® exceed a century.

This naturally leads to questions we will be exploring in this book: why are life-mimicking companies longer-lived and more profitable? Why are they quicker in embracing and creating new technologies? Why are they more adept at connecting with the living world that is their ultimate source of sustenance? And why do they inspire employees to such high levels of productivity?

The answers to these questions are embedded in Figure 1.2.

The longest-lived Global LAMP Index® companies—those that raise the average and median ages of the Index—long ago evolved a moral compass based on the Golden Rule of reciprocity. This predisposed them toward respectful, life-affirming relationships guided by listening to others, learning by their corporate mistakes, and striving to live in harmony with humanity and Nature.

Since the 1970s, as world economies moved into ecological over-step, these companies were among the first to understand that living systems have limits beyond which they cannot go, and they adapted by consciously working to build the awareness and skills to work within those limits.

As reflected in the organic model of Figure 1.2, we find core beliefs that people and Nature are more important than capital assets, and that companies must live in harmony with life if they want to succeed. While many of us associate these beliefs with small community-based companies, they actually thrive in corporate giants such as Unilever, which are becoming important global learning centers.

Consistent with the self-awareness of life-mimicking companies, their visions and values are ecocentric, ethical, imaginative, and inspiring. Unilever's vision of halving the ecological footprint of its products between 2010 and 2020, while improving living conditions in emerging markets, fits this description.

When authentically rooted in company history and culture, such visionary goals can inspire great innovation leaps. Toyota's development of hybrid and zero-emission fuel-cell cars can be traced back to Taiichi Ohno who, between 1948 and 1975, designed the company's famed production system based on cybernetic principles found in Nature. Similarly, Unilever's Sustainable Living Plan is an extension of William Lever's 19th-century concept of responsible capitalism and Floris Maljers' strategic imperatives of sustainable agriculture, sustainable fishing, and clean water.

To companies that mimic life, such learning and innovation come easily. In common with all life, from single cells to large ecosystems, their highly networked systems within systems are acutely sensitive to changes in their operating environments. The cellular organizations of their business units (subsystems), serve as front-line autonomous centers of localized expertise that both inform the whole firm while being served in turn by the financial and embedded intellectual resources of the whole.

Corporate structures based on these principles can therefore be big and small at the same time: big in the scope of their corporate reach, but small in the ways they operate at the local level. This fractal (self-replicating) structure, which is embedded in the very architecture of Nature, enables Unilever to maintain the creative spirit and rewards of small, dedicated work teams while enjoying the synergies of a large resource-rich network.

In describing this model of organization, Unilever calls itself a "multi-local" multinational. With global business units extensively managed by indigenous people, it is highly aware of its many operating environments and, by being so attuned, it is more agile and better able to spot emerging trends.

As one would expect, Unilever's corporate behaviors reflect its vision, values, goals, and organizational structure. Employees, inspired by these values, share a sense of responsibility to future generations and an urgency to lead in reducing the ecological footprint of their products.

Inside the firm, everything is geared to learning. Employees are respected for their individual talents, mentored along their career paths, provided access to critical corporate information and given decision-making authority.

Unilever further extends its life-affirming values and commitment to learning into its supply network. A responsible sourcing policy looks to improve the quality of life in communities along its supply chain, particularly in the developing world. An "open innovation" portal invites suppliers and researchers to collaborate in priority areas—an openness that extends to sharing sustainability insights with competitors. Commenting on these initiatives, Polman says,

"If we achieve our sustainability targets and no one else follows, we will have failed."

> We are stepping up cooperation with suppliers—called Open Innovation—to tap into the best and brightest ideas from outside the company. We are also leveraging our Venture Fund to invest in emerging technologies.
>
> Paul Polman, CEO, Unilever[8]

Reflecting the success of Unilever's outreach to suppliers, it has featured in the global Gartner Supply Chain "top 25" every year since 2009, ranking third in the June 2015 survey.

Good as such exemplary sustainability rankings are, the attribute that maintains Unilever's reinforcing cycle of LAS is profit. By rewarding shareholders and enhancing the firm's ability to raise capital, it is able to maintain its progressive culture and spread its life-affirming ideals. Like the abundance of a healthy forest, profit enables Unilever's culture to thrive and evolve.

As the renowned management consultant, Peter Drucker, famously said, "Profit is not the cause or rationale of business, but rather a test of its validity." In proving the validity of LAS—particularly in comparison with the dying traditional model of the firm—Unilever and the other six companies profiled in this book are changing the course of corporate history.

8   Paul Polman (2010). Speech to Unilever's Annual General Meeting. Retrieved from https://www.unilever.com/Images/paul-polman-agm-speech-2010_tcm244-418634_en.pdf.

Coherence

The strength of Unilever's culture resides in the **coherence between means and ends**. The life-affirming goals of its Sustainable Living Plan are credible to employees and stakeholders precisely because they are achieved by life-affirming means.

This raises an important distinction that will be highlighted throughout this book. Companies that use life-affirming means to accomplish life-affirming goals are said to **manage by means** (MBM). As illustrated by our iceberg diagrams, this is conceptually and functionally very different than traditional management strategies where bottom line results take priority—a practice called **management by results** (MBR).

Qualitatively, companies that authentically practice MBM have a coherent sense of system (defined as the ability to connect and empathize with the larger biospheric and social systems in which they operate). They understand the complexities of relationships and feedbacks that determine outcomes in all life, including companies and markets. Call it a practical ethic: their goals are to live in harmony with people and Nature, which are the sources of their profit.

Companies that practice MBR, on the other hand, have a narrower perspective that too often overrides people and Nature in the singular pursuit of profit. As illustrated in Figure 1.1, such practices create systemic stress which feeds back to poor employee morale, strained customer relationships, and ultimately shorter corporate life expectancies.

Taking MBM to a more personal level: if human intelligence is our most precious resource, we get more of that resource by respecting employees, serving their professional growth, offering them meaningful work, and listening to their ideas than we ever could by directing them to produce numbers of sales, market share, and profit.

The eminent psychologist and business professor, Frederick Herzberg, put it well: "Numbers numb our feelings for what is being counted and lead to adoration of the economies of scale. Passion is in feeling the quality of the experience, not in trying to measure it."

At Unilever the operating leverage of MBM extends far beyond inspiring employees with meaningful work and uplifting visions of sustainable living. As we shall see in the following sections, it also includes the way a company reaches out to customers, local partners, and others in its value-creating network.

Consider, for example, how Unilever simultaneously builds customer loyalty and reduces its ecological footprint through its "Five Levers for Change" advertising strategy.

Unilever's "Five Levers for Change"

Because the environmental impacts of Unilever's products are more pronounced during consumer use than during manufacturing and distribution, its advertising strategy looks to educate people on how to use these products to greatest advantage. The five themes in advertising are, therefore, to:

1. Make it understood

2. Make it easy

3. Make it desirable

4. Make it rewarding

5. Make it a habit

Keith Weed, Chief Marketing and Communication Officer, frames Unilever's outreach to consumers succinctly: "At Unilever, nearly 70% of the greenhouse gas impact of our products occurs when consumers use them to wash their hair or do their laundry."[9] The critical variable here is the energy required to heat water and treat postconsumer waste.

Commenting on the social overhead costs of healthcare, he goes on to say:

> [The] Lifebuoy soap brand, which spearheads our efforts to reduce childhood mortality through the simple act of hand-washing at key hygiene moments throughout the day … is an extremely cost-effective intervention: a $3.35 investment in handwashing brings the same health benefits as an $11 investment in latrine construction, a $200 investment in household water supply and an investment of thousands of dollars in immunisation.

Because half of Unilever's water footprint is associated with consumer use, its advertising shows how its products reduce the need for water in bathing and washing. Its foamless Comfort One Rinse fabric conditioner, for example, requires only a third of the water used in conventional rinsing. This has particular benefits in developing areas where water is scarce and where women spend much of their time procuring water for washing by hand. In more developed markets, the message includes energy savings because washing machines can do their work in shorter cycles.

The overarching theme in Unilever's product design and marketing is how "small actions" can make a "big difference." Because its products are used more than 2 billion times a day, many small changes in consumer behavior—using less energy and water plus

9   Keith Weed (2012, November 6). Change consumer behavior with these five levers. *Harvard Business Review*. Retrieved from http://blogs.hbr.org/2012/11/change-consumer-behavior-with/.

adopting healthy habits around hygiene and nutrition—do indeed add up to important ecological and public health advantages. Likewise, by sourcing these products from local suppliers that use progressive environmental and labor practices, Unilever creates conditions that relieve poverty, reduce CO_2 emissions, and keep money circulating in host communities.

[W]e design products that are used 2 billion times a day ... This means that we play a critical role in [consumers'] behaviour which affects their health and well-being, and the extent to which they impact our planet when carrying out everyday actions. If we can help all our consumers to make small changes in behaviour then, multiplied by billions of uses, this can make a huge difference to our world. Subtle changes in product design can enable these changes.

Richard L. Wright,
Behavioural Science Director, Unilever[10]

Project Shakti

Many of the strategic insights embedded in Unilever's "Five Levers for Change" emerged from earlier experiences with Project Shakti, a marketing experiment launched in India during 2000 by its 67%-owned Hindustan Lever subsidiary.

---

10   Richard L. Wright (n.d.). Technology holds the key to the future. In *Inspiring Sustainable Living: Expert Insights into Consumer Behaviour and Unilever's Five Levers for Change* (pp. 28-31), p. 28. Retrieved from https://www.unilever.com/Images/slp_5-levers-for-change_tcm13-387353_tcm244-409796_en.pdf.

As a collaboration with more than 300 partners—including NGOs, banks, and state and local government—the project initially helped more than 13,000 rural women form self-help groups, receive training in selling and book-keeping, and microcredits so they could become local marketers of Unilever products. This enabled their families, which had formerly relied mainly on the husband's employment, to increase monthly incomes by 50–100%. Beyond the advantage to individual families, the project looked to improve community health and welfare.

Shakti self-help groups—typically 10–15 women from the same village—function as mutual thrift societies. Participating women ("Shakti Ammas") contribute to a common pool of funds buttressed by microcredits from a sponsoring agency. Working capital is used to purchase small affordable sachets of Hindustan Lever products, such as shampoo, hair oil, detergent, skin creams, tea, toothpaste, soap, and water purifier, which would be resold in the community for a 12–15% profit. As a marketing strategy it works from the bottom up rather than the top down. Because local Ammas know customers as neighbors, they have the advantage of familiarity and trust. On promotional "Shakti days" they develop interest in Unilever products via demonstrations and free samples. A communicator ("Vani"), who is an expert on health and hygiene, supports local marketing teams as a resource for teaching and product information.

As additional resources, Shakti entrepreneurs are supported by information kiosks that give local villages free access to interactive voice-enabled computers offering information on education, employment, agriculture, pest control, animal husbandry, health, personal care, and legal procedures. Users of these Shakti portals can post queries on these subjects to local experts who generally respond within 48 hours.

In 2010, Hindustan Lever expanded the program to include men ("Shaktimaans"), who were provided with bicycles to distribute products to nearby villages. By year-end 2013, 65,000 Shakti Ammas and 30,000 Shaktimaans were selling products to over 3 million households in 100,000 Indian villages.

Conceptually, the Shakti approach is grounded in systems thinking: using the local knowledge of thousands of people who have a natural interest in the health of their families and communities, enabling that knowledge to spread through Vanis and localized information kiosks, and using whole system feedbacks to advance the wellbeing of people in the system.

To C.K. Pralahad, author of the business classic, *The Fortune at the Bottom of the Pyramid*, Project Shakti created a new business system that helped Hindustan Unilever gain significant market share in a short period of time. By working collaboratively with NGOs, governments, and other groups committed to reducing poverty, the company made important inroads into "dark" areas of the market that were difficult to reach due to poor transportation and communications infrastructure. Further, by addressing these markets in a symbiotic way based on mutual advantage, Hindustan Unilever achieved a win–win goal of reducing poverty, expanding its market, and accelerating profit.

Based on its success, the Shakti model is now being replicated in Pakistan and Sri Lanka, where there are now thousands of locally engaged entrepreneurs. By year-end 2015, Unilever further spread these practices to Africa.

We are now sourcing more than half our agricultural raw materials sustainably and have reached
around 800,000 smallholder farmers with help
and training. We have created 70,000 women
micro-entrepreneurs distributing our products in
India while making progress on our new commitments to enhance livelihoods across the value
chain.

Unilever Annual Report, 2014[11]

Engaging the whole system

The magic of Unilever's strategy—and the reason it is a global sustainability and profit leader—resides in continuously engaging the
whole system in which it operates. Rather than treating each challenge as a "one-off" or, worse, sinking into a self-congratulatory
sense of accomplishment, it habitually looks for new leverage
points.

A case in point is Unilever's goal, announced in 2010, to source
all its palm oil sustainably from certified, traceable sources by 2020
while using its knowledge and influence to get the world's large suppliers and buyers to join in its quest. Like its open innovation portal, the company knows it can do more in partnership with others
than it can do alone.

11   Unilever (2014). *Annual Report and Accounts 2014: Strategic Report,*
     p. 11. Retrieved from https://www.unilever.com/Images/ara-2014-strategic
     -report_tcm244-421153_en.pdf.

As one of the world's most diverse agricultural commodities—used in making food products, cosmetics, shampoos, detergents, and biofuels—palm oil accounts for more than two-thirds of all internationally traded vegetable oil. Over the past 40 years, cultivation has increased faster than any other major type of food or industrial agricultural crop. Likewise, per capita human consumption of vegetable oil has increased more rapidly during the past 30 years than any other food.

At stake in this profusion of palm oil production and consumption are vast tracts of tropical rainforest in Africa, Indonesia, Malaysia, and Latin America, whose biodiversity and water systems are essential resources to billions of people, and whose carbon-absorbing capacity is a strategic antidote to global climate change.

For years, opportunists have been cutting and burning these essential habitats to make room for palm oil plantations. Worse, the carbon emissions from burning cleared forestland have increased the risks of climate change and threatened local food systems—a lose–lose proposition for the biosphere, humanity, regional prosperity, and ultimately the world economy.

By getting other business leaders to see this calamity as a systemic challenge, Paul Polman reckoned he could effect change that would serve all players. So he formed a working group through the 400-company Global Consumer Goods Forum to study the matter. By sharing data on inconvenient facts and on the opportunities of amending the world's degraded land, he convinced a critical mass of corporate peers to sign on, including Wilmar, the world's largest supplier of palm oil.

Polman recently stated:

> Deforestation is not one of the great challenges in the fight against climate change, it is the most important and most immediate and most urgent challenge ... Most CEOs are convinced or now know that their companies cannot prosper in

a world of runaway climate change, and that's increasingly becoming evident … Above all, these business leaders recognize that the cost of inaction is actually rapidly becoming greater than the cost of action.[12]

Polman's credibility in convincing the world's largest buyers and suppliers of palm oil to change their practices owed much to his success at Unilever in turning sustainability into a value-added venture rather than a cost. Today, the Roundtable on Sustainable Palm Oil, which Polman initiated, has over 2,700 members. Included among the major consumer goods companies signing on are Colgate Palmolive, Conagra, Danone, Henkel, Mars, Nestlé, Johnson & Johnson, Kellogg's, Kraft, L'Oreal, Procter & Gamble, Reckitt Benckiser, and Quaker.

Polman describes this buy-in as a "race to the top," a moment of enlightenment that in itself, as an awakening to systems thinking, has extraordinary leverage potential toward changing other corporate behaviors.[13]

A global moment of truth

Unilever's story is the subject of this chapter because it shows us a way forward in a world of narrowing options. As illuminated by our iceberg diagrams, companies are today faced with two strategic alternatives:

12   Bruno Vander Velde (2014, December 8). Unilever CEO: deforestation is the most urgent climate challenge. *Forests News*. Retrieved from http://blog.cifor.org/25716/ceo-governments-private-sector-must-work-in-tandem-to-tackle-most-urgent-challenge?fnl=en.

13   Unilever (2014, September 23). First global timeline to end forest loss welcomed. Retrieved from https://www.unilever.com/news/press-releases/2014/14-09-23-First-global-timeline-to-end-forest-loss-welcomed.html.

1. The **win–win strategy** of biomimicry and LAS

2. The **lose–lose strategy** of the collapsing industrial capitalist model

Given the alarming realities of global climate change, ecological
overstep, compounding debt/GDP ratios, out-of-control derivatives
speculation, and social fragmentation, business as usual has no
future. Considered in this context, Unilever offers us a compelling
way forward.

Among forward-thinking corporate leaders, especially those who
awakened during the 2008 global economic crisis, there is a hunger
for transformative new ideas as the ecological sources of that crisis
become more apparent. In the chapters that follow we will explore
the best of these ideas and how they evolved, through the stories of
our exemplary Focus Group leaders.

The choice between win–win and lose–lose is, of course, stark.
There is little room for temporizing. LAS cannot be bolted onto a
traditional business organization. The two cultures are radically
different. They would clash.

The new reality for traditionally managed companies is that their
lives are on the line. They must adapt, and adapt quickly, or risk
losing valuable employees, customers, and market share.

This choice, however, need not be stultifying. The important
thing for leaders is to be clear and truthful about the need to change
course. Truth-telling has a salubrious effect. Employees respect it.
When combined with processes of shared visioning and brainstorming, it releases a torrent of creative energy. People want to find
meaning in their work, something that awakens their passions and
makes their lives worthwhile.

The secret of life-mimicking companies is the awakening of these
very human passions. As modern science explores the frontiers of
human consciousness and creativity, we now see more clearly the

leverage of engaging those passions. As catalysts of human creativity and innovation, they are far more powerful than mechanistic leverage ever was.

Like the European Renaissance 600 years ago, we have reached a turning point in human understanding and evolution. And there will be no going back.

2

The power of the network

Whenever we look at life, we look at networks.

Fritjof Capra[1]

The way to a happier and more prosperous state is clear: Concede once and for all that employees, not managers, are the true engines of progress, and dedicate your career to creating an environment in which employees can stretch for higher and higher levels of performance.

Ken Iverson, CEO, Nucor[2]

1   Fritjof Capra (1997). *The Web of Life: A New Scientific Understanding of Living Systems*. New York, NY: First Anchor Books, p. 82. Reproduced by kind permission of Fritjof Capra.
2   Ken Iverson (1997). *Plain Talk: Lessons from a Business Maverick*. Hoboken, NJ: John Wiley, p. 98.

Imagine a company whose share price rose more than 400-fold while its once largest competitors sank into bankruptcy—a feat it accomplished by radically altering the traditional culture of the deep cyclical, lay-off-prone steel industry. Consider too how it did this with no lay-offs due to lack of work while making many of its blue-collar employees wealthy and sending their children through college on company scholarships. Such is the case of Nucor in the four decades between 1975 and 2015.

Nucor accomplished this feat by transforming its organizational structure from the autocratic top-down norm of the steel industry into a collaborative employee-centered web of information networks. It was, in every sense of the word, a Copernican revolution. Whereas top executives in its industry thought of themselves as the creative center, Nucor took the opposite approach and put employees at the center.

By this single stroke—which implicitly recognizes the firm as a living entity—Nucor created a culture of shared values, deep loyalty, committed teamwork, and exceptional creativity. With no engineering or R&D department it became the innovation and green leader of the global steel industry simply by harnessing the creative insights of frontline workers.

Ken Iverson, the man who turned Nucor around, sensed the power of culture and living networks long before the business and academic mainstream. The system he created mimicked the self-organizing, energy-efficient, resilient processes of Nature in the way it coordinated information and effort. Employees were allowed to experiment, create their own work schedules, and allocate responsibilities based on knowledge of each other's skills and the work to be done. The spontaneity of these team-based networks released a continuous flow of information, fresh insights, and innovations that percolated up through mill networks into a shared corporate network. Unlike the cumbersome top-down bureaucracies of traditionally managed steel companies, Nucor's bottom-up approach was flexible and nimble.

At the time Nucor began its stunning surge to leadership, the conventional wisdom among steelmakers was that only top management had the intelligence to run a successful operation. Since the inception of mass-produced steel in America during the 1870s, managers assumed the thinking capacities, and often the intentions, of millworkers could not be trusted. Proceeding from this mind-set, the processes, rules, and procedures they designed were largely preemptive: aimed to solve problems before they arose so that employees would never have to make decisions. Every step along the production line was carefully controlled and run by the book.

The chief deficiency in this preemptive system was its reliance on hindsight. As new problems arose, rules had to be rewritten. Consequently, by the time Nucor began its stunning ascent in the 1970s, traditional steel mill procedures were often so complex, rigid, and bloated that employees were limited in what they could do.

One of the critical differences between Nucor's approach and those of traditionally run steel companies can be found in the ways they thought of "lines." Traditionalists described lines in terms of one-way arrows: "production lines," where every step was carefully orchestrated, measured, and controlled from mine to factory to warehouse to customer. Iverson's genius was to think in terms of more fluid "front lines," where employees would be more closely connected to each other as well as to suppliers, strategic partners, and customers. By his definition, the front line was to be a permeable boundary (like a living membrane) rather than a defined channel with restricted entry; and it assumed that engaged employees would naturally do the right thing.

The differences between these two approaches to management are summarized in Table 2.1. The attitudes and qualities attributed

TABLE 2.1   Differences between autocratic and employee-centered management models

Autocratic, top-down model	Employee-centered, networked model
• Company is a profit-driven machine	• Company is a values-driven living organism
• Ideals are centered on profit	• Ideals are centered on life (people, Nature)
• Organization is rigidly hierarchical	• Organization is decentralized, localized
• Leaders rule by command and control	• Leaders serve the growth of employees
• Authority is based on rank	• Authority is based on knowledge, experience
• Information is jealously guarded	• Information is widely shared (open book)
• Bureaucratic boundaries are strict	• Boundaries are fluid, permeable
• Employees are told what to do	• Employees can self-organize, experiment
• Production lines define work order	• Frontline employees create own order
• Employees are expendable, costs	• Employees are valuable living assets
• Lay-offs (a first resort) protect profit	• Lay-offs are a last resort
Feedback effects	
• Low employee morale, engagement	• High employee morale, engagement
• Low trust slows communication	• High trust facilitates communication, learning
• Productivity is suboptimal	• Productivity excels

to each model are more inclinations than absolutes. Take hierarchy, for example: while there is some degree of hierarchy in all companies, in highly networked ones, such as Nucor, there are fewer layers between CEO and frontline employees, and decision-making authority is localized rather than centralized at the top.

Nucor was selected for this case study precisely because it pioneered a self-organizing, networked, employee-centered model in an industry renowned for its autocratic, top-down style of management. On the strength of this model, it became the productivity and stewardship leader of its industry and set standards that later were to be widely emulated among other life-mimicking companies.

While some believe the networking model is best suited to highly educated workers, Nucor—whose employees are primarily blue-collar—shows us that networks built on shared life-affirming values and goals work brilliantly wherever they operate. To Iverson, the key was to treat all people as equals. He believed that if you hire good people, treat them with respect, help them grow, vest them in the firm's success and inspire them with an uplifting vision of the future, they will naturally organize themselves in productive ways regardless of formal education; and in this belief he was strikingly correct. As the Nobel laureate, Linus Pauling, famously put it, "The best way to have a good idea is to have lots of ideas."

> [T]he company supplies the equipment, training, benefits program, and other fundamental support, and leaves the rest up to the group. So, in a sense, each group is in business for itself. Work groups set their own goals for exceeding the baseline and work out their own ways of pursuing them, guided only by this certainty: The more they produce, the more they earn.
>
> Ken Iverson, CEO, Nucor[3]

3   Ken Iverson (1997). *Plain Talk: Lessons from a Business Maverick*. Hoboken, NJ: John Wiley, p. 107.

Nucor's founding principles

Although Iverson never spoke of employees and Nature as being living assets, he treated them that way. During his tenure as CEO (1965–98), this was evident both in Nucor's approach to steelmaking and in its care for employees.

Iverson's ideal of steelmaking was to create a network of energy-efficient mini-mills that would feed on recycled scrap—a major departure from the norm of mega-mills, whose energy-hungry blast furnaces fed on resources extracted from the Earth in often harmful ways. Preference in mill siting was given to towns and rural areas— tight-knit communities where people cared for one another and their shared environment.

To show his respect for employees, Iverson made them partners in Nucor's success—a major break from the industry norm of treating them like disposable factors of production. Millworkers were entitled to bonuses every pay period based on their team's production. With no upper limit on bonus payments, they usually earn between 100 and 220% of base salary and average 170–180%.

Further to Iverson's partnership ideal, health benefits were to be the same for everyone—from the CEO to the front line. During periods of slack steel demand, rather than laying people off, everyone takes a pay cut with executives taking the largest percentage cuts. Correspondingly, during boom times, 10% of year-end earnings are allocated to employee profit sharing with additional sums retained on Nucor's balance sheet so it will have the resources to support employees when the cycle reverses.

The logic of such caring is simple. By keeping mills open and work teams together, Nucor creates a virtuous cycle of employee commitment, knowledge sharing, customer service, and repeat business, the result of which is continual market share gains.

To support this life-affirming culture of respect, Iverson created a leadership team that was lean and committed to serving the growth of employees. Unlike most top-heavy Fortune 500 bureaucracies, there were only four levels between the CEO and those on the front line (today there are five). When hot steel is being poured, there is no hierarchy. The people in charge are those with the most knowledge of the task.

To encourage entrepreneurship at all levels, each mill was run like a separate business. The role of the mill manager was to connect with employees in a spirit of listening and mentoring. The goal was to: "help the people you manage to accomplish extraordinary things ... relying on employees to make important decisions and take significant risks ... shaping a work environment that stimulates people to explore their own potential."[4]

Transparent information sharing was a critical part of this management approach. The ideal was to show employees how they and their teams contributed to the success of their mill and the company as a whole. Beyond linking them to their production bonuses, this openness reinforced Nucor's spirit of partnership and a sense of shared destiny.

As founding principles, these partnership ideals became a formidable source of energy. From the time Iverson introduced Nucor's information sharing and incentive plans in 1966, the company has been profitable every year, except 2009, with no lay-offs due to lack of work—a record unmatched in the steel industry. Further, in spite of having the highest-paid workers in the steel industry, Nucor normally has the highest net profit per employee.

Simply put, the new model works because it merges the interests of employees/partners and management in ways the old hierarchical

4   Ibid., p. 23.

model never could. By so engaging employees, Iverson created a force of Nature.

The Golden Rule of reciprocity

Like all competent life-mimicking companies, Nucor's life-affirming culture is based on the Golden Rule of reciprocity. Iverson stated it clearly in his book, *Plain Talk*: "We believe in treating people the way you'd want to be treated. That's a fundamental building block of our company. It sounds simplistic, but it works."[5]

The Golden Rule at Nucor starts with employees' health and safety. For decades, safety has been the top agenda item at every work group, mill, and corporate meeting and everyone is held responsible—not just those specifically charged with overseeing mill operations. A company-wide intranet keeps information continuously flowing on safety tips, accident and injury reviews, and safety success stories. Things that are normally ignored at other companies, such as employee back or joint pain, are studied by in-house medical staff and quickly remediated. At most plants, shifts begin with a daily safety huddle. New employees aren't allowed to work on a line until they are thoroughly familiar with working conditions and safety procedures. Those involved in accidents must give oral reports to their team and the mill's safety unit.

While this approach may seem a waste of time or extravagant to linear thinking, cost-driven companies, it pays for itself in employee goodwill. With injury and illness rates 55–80% below industry averages, Nucor recaptures every dollar it spends on health and safety in employee morale and productivity.

5   Ibid., p. 76.

In 2013 occupational injury and illness rates at Nucor per 100 workers were far below industry averages: 1.44 vs. 3.20 on average at steel mills; 1.69 vs. 7.40 on average at fabricators; and 1.50 vs. 7.00 on average at buildings group facilities.

Nucor Sustainability Report, 2013[6]

The Golden Rule at Nucor is also expressed in its long-standing rules of fair play: "Teammates should feel confident that if they do their jobs properly, they will have a job tomorrow," that they "have a right to be treated fairly and must believe they will," and that they can "ask for a review of a complaint if they feel a supervisor has not provided a fair hearing," with an appeal process all the way up to the corporate office.[7] These words are holy writ at Nucor and consistently honored. Because employees believe in them, they feel more free to exchange information, experiment and think creatively.

Nucor's concern for the wellbeing of employees was particularly evident during the recession of 2008 and 2009, when demand for steel fell sharply and the company lost money. Instead of laying off people, as other companies did, it used the downtime to upgrade mill facilities, boost energy efficiency, cross-train workers, and perform maintenance so it would be better positioned to prosper in the next upturn. (Conversely, in 2007, when profits were more robust, Nucor placed $220 million into profit sharing for millworkers, which worked out to about $8,000 per employee.)

6   Nucor (2013). *Nucor Sustainability Report 2013*, p. 10. Retrieved from http://www.nucor.com/sustainability/2013/download/Nucor_Sustainability Report13.pdf.

7   Nucor (2016). Our story. Chapter 4: culture. Retrieved from http://www. nucor.com/story/chapter4/.

To the small towns and rural areas where most of Nucor's mills are located, these policies keep money circulating in host communities to the benefit of local businesses and municipalities. In addition to the security this provides, Nucor mills support local schools, fire departments, disaster relief, and environmental projects with donations and volunteer time. As a result, having a job at Nucor is widely considered an honor—a source of pride that increases the desire of employees to serve and create. Because of this, Nucor maintains an exceptionally high employee retention rate (93% in 2013), which stabilizes work teams and enhances collegiality.

Nucor's scholarship programs further deepen these bonds of reciprocal caring. Children of employees get up to $3,000 per year for four years at accredited colleges. Employees themselves can get up to $3,000 per year of tuition reimbursement for approved courses and their spouses can get up to $1,500 per year for a maximum of two years.

In all these dimensions, Nucor's concern for the health of the whole ecosystem in which it exists is the polar opposite of Big Steel with its privileged executive class and its "us vs. them" approach to labor.

What Iverson liked about the Golden Rule was its simplicity, fairness, and practicality. It didn't require complex written manuals or layers of middle managers to supervise—just common sense and decency. More importantly, it leveraged the natural instincts of people to network, learn, and experiment toward common goals, which have so powerfully lifted Nucor's market share and profits.

From deep caring to deep thinking

While Iverson saw such deep caring as a matter of common sense and decency, it is in fact supported by the logic of modern neuroscience. As mentioned in the Introduction, companies that empathize with employees and affiliate with their ideals and deep values touch the powerful gut–heart–brain networks that engage their highest (quantum) thinking capacities.

In systems thinking terms, these inner neural networks are gateways to the higher-thinking capacities of employees, which enriches both work teams and the company as a whole. Physiologically, such networks link the executive part of our brains to the neurology of our hearts and guts, which guide the brain by investing it with instinctive senses of meaning, value, and direction. In a very real sense, this internal neural networking is where the more interactive networking between people begins.

To the renowned Harvard biologist, Edward O. Wilson, the instincts that arise from these neural networks are rooted in our biophilic "affinity with life"—a quality that has been wired into our DNA over thousands of generations because individuals who respected life lived longer and thus had more opportunities to pass on their genes.[8]

Although Iverson never used words like spiritual intelligence, he trusted that deeply cared-for employees would deeply care about Nucor, that life-affirming goals would inspire great effort, and that people so inspired could be trusted to do the right thing. Consequently, in a bold leap of faith—unimaginable to the command-and-control hierarchies of conventionally managed steel companies—he empowered Nucor millworkers to organize their

8   Edward O. Wilson (1984). *Biophilia*. Cambridge, MA: Harvard University Press.

own work teams, to set their own schedules, and to experiment freely with ideas and insights without fear of failure or criticism.

By virtually any standard, this trusting leap was a resounding success. The ideas and insights that spontaneously arose from the floors of these mills made Nucor an innovation hothouse. That is why, with no engineering or R&D department, it quickly became a global technology leader—setting new standards for employee productivity, product quality, industrial ecology, energy efficiency, and low greenhouse gas emissions.

Our people excel because they are allowed to fail. It's why our managers encourage their teammates to try out their new ideas. Given respect and control, Nucor teammates don't need a memo to get going. It's this freedom to try that gives us one of the most creative, get-it-done workforces in the world.

Nucor, "Our story"[9]

To keep this deep-caring, deep-thinking environment alive, Iverson created a culture of promoting from within and cultivated people who shared that belief. What he sought were people who would become stewards of Nucor's values rather than charismatic, self-absorbed leaders. His successors as CEO—John Correnti (1999), Dan DiMicco (2000–12) and John Ferriola (2013–present)—all came up through the mill system and served under Iverson. Except for a board coup in 1999, which briefly threatened to derail Nucor's culture, these successor CEOs have guarded the firm's core

---

9   Nucor (2016). Our story. Chapter 4: culture. Retrieved from http://www. nucor.com/story/chapter4/.

values and decentralized, networked structure, which have been so popular with employees.

Relational equity

It is hard to overstate the values of caring and mutual trust in a corporate network. In Nucor's case, caring and trust derive from reciprocal relationships, where people serve one another in pursuit of common goals. The strength of those relationships defines Nucor's **relational equity**—both within the firm and in its outreach to customers and other stakeholders. As will be demonstrated throughout this book, relational equity is an exceptionally reliable (yet often overlooked) leading indicator of financial equity.

Indeed, Iverson's knack for generating relational equity was the catalyst by which Nucor transformed itself from a failing, near-bankrupt company into America's largest, most profitable steel producer. In 1965, when he became CEO of Nuclear Corporation of America (later shortened to Nucor), the firm had only $21 million in annual sales, equivalent to less than two days of US Steel's turnover. By the time Iverson retired in 1998, however, Nucor's market capitalization was larger than that of US Steel.

How did this happen? Broadly speaking, Iverson achieved this turnaround by putting a higher value on living assets than on nonliving capital assets—in effect, reversing steel company norms. By making employees the center of Nucor's universe rather than treating them as disposables as US Steel did, he won their loyalty and trust. By caring about their families and communities, they, in turn, cared for the company and its customers. By reinventing the steel industry around eco-efficient mini-mills (more on this later), he inspired them to think creatively and to continuously push innovation.

Looking back on Nucor's trajectory since introducing these changes, it was like jumping from Neanderthal to modern man in a generation. Because the new mills were smarter, nimbler, and more energetic than the old integrated mills, they quickly made quantum jumps in innovation, cost-effectiveness, and survivability. Their competitive advantages were such that, barely a decade after Nucor opened its first mini-mill (1969), the company was a global innovation leader, ultimately forcing US Steel and other large steelmakers into mergers and divestitures. Between 1997 and 2001, no less than 29 American steel companies entered bankruptcy.[10]

To put an exclamation point on this turnaround, Nucor's extraordinary shareholder returns were accomplished during a time (1967–2015) when gross production of the U.S. steel industry declined 31% from 115 to 79 million tonnes per year. Although its technology was a factor in this extraordinary period, Nucor's main advantage resided in its relational equity with employees, which made possible that technology and the company's legendary work ethic.

Even though US Steel and others have over the past few decades closed much of the technology gap, Nucor retains its productivity edge thanks to its stronger relational equity with employees. This was evident during 2015, a terrible year for the steel industry with demand shriveling and prices falling to 12-year lows. During that period Nucor's revenue per employee ($696,610) was more than double that of US Steel ($312,703). More importantly, it remained profitable with a positive net income of $358 million while US Steel suffered a loss of $1.5 billion due to a series of plant closures and asset write-downs.

10   Gary Clyde Hufbauer & Ben Goodrich (2002, January). Time for a Grand Bargain in Steel? Retrieved from https://piie.com/publications/policy-briefs/time-grand-bargain-steel.

Sense of system

One of the key advantages of Nucor's relational equity is the way it fosters an enlightened **sense of system**. The company harvests a continuous flow of feedback from customers and other stakeholders through empowered and entrepreneurial frontline employees that both deepens its understanding of its business ecosystem and enables it to sense changes ahead of competitors.

That sensing capacity was clearly evident in 2015, when Nucor earned a profit while the global steel industry was in a deep recession. It is also a primary reason why Nucor has been profitable in all but one of the 50 years between 1965 and 2015.

As we shall see in subsequent chapters, when companies develop a coherent sense of system they become more aware of the limits and potentials of their corporate ecosystems, which reside in people and Nature. This insight also enables them to steward more effectively the true sources of their knowledge and value creation.

Long before such ecocentric concepts became popular in business journals and academic papers, Ken Iverson embedded them in Nucor's culture. In fact, when asked the secret to Nucor's success, his stock reply was: "It is 70% culture and 30% technology."

Looking back to Nucor's stunning turnaround in 1965, we see clear evidence of this pattern. Rather than mimicking the failing culture of traditionally run steel companies, he devised a biomimetic system that replicated Nature's time-tested patterns and strategies. Prominent among these were his beliefs that mill employees could effectively **self-organize** without supervision, that their **symbiotic** concern for teammates would make time clocks unnecessary, and that their natural **instincts to learn and adapt** would generate **synergies** that leverage productivity.

We find further evidence of biomimicry in Iverson's efforts to **minimize entropy** via energy-efficient recycling methods, which reduce the ecological footprint and unnecessary waste of steelmaking. It is also evident in Nucor's frugal self-financing culture, which minimizes disruptive financial risk.

In a broader sense, the attribute for which Nucor is best known—Iverson's introduction of the mini-mill—reflects the **fractal organization** of Nature. Long before fractals became a topic of academic interest in the 1990s, Iverson imagined Nucor as a series of networks (work teams) within networks (mini-mills) that reside within a larger corporate network, where all play by the same rules of individual respect and openness, enabling information to flow freely where needed as it does in Nature.

Like the cell structure of the human body, which is infused with a shared DNA, there can be incredible diversity and specialization within such architecture. Because each work team and mini-mill is subtly different (based on differences in personnel, customer demand, workflow, etc.), the fractal system is quick to sense changes in local conditions. As that local feedback is distributed and processed through mill and corporate information systems, the whole organization learns and adapts—effectively becoming more than the sum of its parts.

As Iverson saw it, this model enabled employees to operate efficiently with fewer managers. Because most operating decisions are made at the division level or lower, and frontline workers are empowered to innovate, Nucor today works with a lean corporate staff of only 95 people (including clerical employees). With a total employment of more than 23,600, that works out to one corporate staffer per 250 workers.

Like the corporate structure of Unilever, the fractal configuration of Nucor's mini-mill system enables the company to be big and small at the same time. Within each mill, employees know one another on a first-name basis, the plant manager's door is always open, and everyone has a stake in the mill's success.

Beyond that collegiality, the glue that holds the system together is a cultural DNA of shared ideals and values that keep everyone working for the good of the greater whole. Today these are expressed in Nucor's goal to be: "cultural and environmental stewards" while also being "the safest, highest quality, lowest cost, most productive and most profitable steel and steel products company in the world."[11]

The eco-inspired mini-mill model

Nucor opened its first mini-mill in 1969—four years after Ken Iverson became CEO. By year-end 2015, it had 24 minis plus two micromills, each operating on similar organizational principles. As their names imply, these are small facilities, most of which are located near to their sources of supply (scrap steel) and end markets.

In keeping with their fractal structures, each mill is effectively a learning lab, where employees are empowered to experiment and where best ideas are quickly shared through the larger corporate network.

Since each mill is run as a separate business, where employee bonuses are tied to mill success, and where employee families live nearby, the interests of all who serve in the mill are perfectly aligned. That sense of shared destiny, seconded by a fierce pride in Nucor's innovative culture, has made it the global sustainability and profit leader in steelmaking for more than four decades.

The eco-effectiveness of Nucor's mini-mill strategy and culture are reflected in its results. By the company's reckoning, for every ton of steel produced, its mills save in relation to traditional mega-mills:

11   U.S. Green Building Council (2016). Nucor Corporation. Retrieved from http://www.usgbc.org/organizations/nucor-corporation.

- 2,500 pounds of iron ore
- 1,400 pounds of coal
- 120 pounds of limestone
- 1,705 kWh of electricity

Multiply that by the 19.3 million tons of steel produced in 2015 and the resource and monetary savings are immense.[12]

Further, Nucor's electric arc furnaces reportedly release 86 fewer pounds of pollutants into the air for every ton of steel produced relative to the coal furnaces of integrated mills. Over the course of one year, that has the effect of reducing particulate matter emissions by over 2 million tons. Taken together, Nucor says its mini-mills "reduce mining waste by 97%, air pollution by 86%, & water pollution by 76%."[13]

In a further step toward eco-efficiency, Nucor's new micro-mill technology makes ultra-thin, flat rolled steel in a one-step (Castrip®) process with 84% less energy than a conventional mill, plus a 75% reduction in greenhouse gas emissions. Because Castrip® mills can be located on 50-acre lots—1% of the space needed for an integrated mill—they can be sited close to their customers, reducing transportation costs and emissions.

With each step toward such efficiencies, Nucor reduces its costs of operation and strengthens demand for its products, leading to increased profit margins and financial security. Because employees see these connections and are rewarded for their innovations, they eagerly contribute to advancing Nucor's environmental leadership.

---

12 Nucor reports its production in short tons (2,000 pounds), as do all U.S. manufacturers.

13 Nucor (n.d.). *Sustainability of Nucor Building Systems*, p. 4. Retrieved from http://www.nucorbuildingsystems.com/builder/Secure/pdf_files/ppt-sustainability.pptx.

Nucor's Darlington, South Carolina mini-mill exemplifies this system. Thanks to the innovative ideas of frontline employees, this million-ton-per-year steelmaking plant:

- Collects, cools, treats, and recycles 35,000 gallons of water per minute

- Extracts and resells 20 tons per day of zinc from furnace dust

- Recycles 150,000 tons of slag per year for use in building roads

- Reprocesses and sells 14,000 tons of mill scale per year as an ingredient for making Portland cement

- Reclaims the oils used in plant machinery and trucks

- Recycles office equipment, packaging, and other wastes

As Nucor learns to become more eco-efficient and profitable through its mini-mill network, it consistently raises the bar on performance. Today, the main focus of its environmental stewardship is to reduce the life-cycle impacts of its products and processes. To accomplish this, in 2009 it undertook a complete cradle-to-cradle assessment of its bar, beam, plate, and sheet steel production processes—from the environmental impacts of mill production, to the ways its products and raw materials were shipped, to how its products are used, and to how they are recycled at the end of their useful lives.

Although this advanced concept of closed-cycle management arose long after Iverson retired as CEO, his successors have continually supported Nucor's founding principles. In a very real sense, they understand, as Iverson did, that Nucor is more than a steel company. In its organizational structure, information sharing, and visionary mission to be "cultural and environmental stewards," it has become a vibrant learning center seeking more harmonious ways of doing business on an ecologically stressed planet.

In this way, Nucor has powerfully demonstrated the reinforcing cycle of living asset stewardship (LAS). Other companies may copy its mini-mill methods of production but, until they achieve its eco-centric culture and the binding power of its values, they are unlikely to match its productivity.

Centrality of values

As mentioned earlier, Nucor's values, ideals, and goals are its cultural DNA—the qualities that bind its fractal organization into a coherent whole and keep its many moving parts from spinning off into chaos.

Beyond sharing similar values and goals (to make Nucor "cultural and environmental stewards"), managers and employees want to build a great corporation, to be part of something they can be proud of. Mills are infused with rich social networks as employees bond, cross-train, and help one another. Given Nucor's culture of caring and sharing, where leaders are always accessible, communications are typically informal and familial.

The easygoing and inspirational nature of these qualities makes employees feel special and ignites their desire to experiment and innovate. The Dartmouth/Tuck professor, Vijay Govindarajan, a renowned authority on leadership and innovation, calls this collective spirit Nucor's "emotional infrastructure."[14]

---

14   Vijay Govindarajan & Subroto Bagchi (2009). The emotionally bonded organization: why emotional infrastructure matters and how leaders can build it. Retrieved from http://www.tuck.dartmouth.edu/people/vg/blog-archive/EBO-2009.pdf.

Because Nucor's emotional infrastructure is the source of the company's greatest achievements, it is a consideration in all strategic decision-making. Were that not the case, the company's values, ideals, and goals would become mere window dressing and would generate cynicism, rather than pride and creative energy, among employees.

The care Nucor takes in protecting its cultural DNA and emotional infrastructure was clearly evident in its 2008 acquisition of the David J. Joseph Company (DJJ)—a 20 million ton/year scrap metal business with whom Nucor had been doing business since 1970. Nucor's decision to acquire DJJ was not primarily driven by size as so many corporate mergers are, but hinged instead on cultural affinity.

Like Nucor, DJJ was decentralized and highly networked. Local business units had autonomy, which enabled them to know their customers and to act entrepreneurially. Importantly, both companies were leaders in the American recycling movement with cultures based on care for employees, the environment, and host communities. Both also took pride in their financial integrity and their ability to survive hard times (DJJ actually expanded its business during the Great Depression of the 1930s). The care that DJJ took to separate hazardous substances from its semifinished products was especially important to Nucor, which put a high premium on employee safety.

To Nucor CEO Dan DiMicco, who consummated the deal, the cultural fit was ideal. Having known each other at the corporate and local levels for 38 years, the two firms were like old friends. They already had *de facto* networks in place, secured by a history of good communication, shared values, and trust. The only thing that remained to be done was to formalize what had evolved informally.

Compared with Mittal's 2006 global acquisition drive to become the world's largest steel producer, Nucor's acquisition of DJJ may seem modest, but it has been accretive, trouble-free, and a positive to Nucor's balance sheet.

By comparison, Mittal (now ArcelorMittal) too often ignored cultural matters in its quest for bulk. As a result, it has been forced into multiple divestitures in order to repair its balance sheet. Reflecting these developments, Nucor's market capitalization at year-end 2015 ($13 billion) was roughly 62% higher than that of ArcelorMittal ($8 billion), in spite of the fact that ArcelorMittal's revenues were 3½ times larger.

Soft power

Say what you will about visionary goals, emotional infrastructure, spiritual intelligence, and the importance of uplifting corporate values, corporate networks run most effectively on soft power.

Iverson got this. By approaching Nucor's future in a holistic ecocentric context, rather than the more traditional bottom-line-first context, he and his successors developed its networking capacity in ways that physical infrastructure and numbers-driven cultures never could.

Stated differently, Iverson understood that managing by means (MBM) has advantages over managing by results (MBR) because informed and inspired people are the means by which companies fulfill their potential.

The systems thinker, Donella Meadows, sums it up well: "Visionary human intentions can bring forth not only new information, new feedback loops, new behavior, new knowledge and new technology, but also new institutions, new physical structures, and new powers within human beings."[15]

15   Donella Meadows, Jorgen Randers, & Dennis Meadows (2004). *Limits to Growth: The 30-Year Update*. White River Junction, VT: Chelsea Green, p. 272.

Although her comment was general, not one about Nucor *per se*, it distills in a few words what Iverson accomplished. It also leads us coherently into forthcoming chapters because networks are the foundation of all life and, by extension, of companies that mimic life.

In building up from this vantage point, Chapters 3–7 cover each of five other attributes of life that strengthen and empower networks. The last of these, consciousness, is an emergent quality that becomes more developed as companies become more lifelike.

There is an elegant symmetry to this. It has evolved over billions of years and will continue to evolve so long as we, who possess this quality of consciousness, use it wisely. For the truth is: profit can only come from life, in which case profit must ultimately serve to sustain life.

3

Management by means

> [A] company that manages by means will profit
> only by nurturing fundamental human and natu-
> ral relationships, in contrast to the convention-
> ally managed company that drives people to
> meet profit targets by sacrificing human and nat-
> ural relationships.
>
> H. Thomas Johnson and Anders Broms[1]

> Our goal is to have the best educated workforce
> on the planet.
>
> George David, Chairman and CEO, UTC[2]

1   H. Thomas Johnson & Anders Broms (2000). *Profit Beyond Measure: Extraordinary Results Through Attention to Work and People*. New York, NY: The Free Press, p. 7.

2   Tyya N. Turner *et al.* (Eds.) (2005). *Vault Guide to the Top Manufacturing Employers*. New York, NY: Vault, p. 263.

In 1996, the United Technologies Corporation (UTC) launched its employee scholar program (ESP), which enables employees to obtain a degree in any field, whether or not it is job-related, with full reimbursement for tuition, academic fees, and course-required books. Degrees in history, philosophy, or the arts were as valid as those in mathematics, engineering, and business. The idea was to ignite a passion for learning that would carry over to UTC's higher life-affirming goals.

All full- and part-time employees are eligible for the ESP up to and including PhD degrees, and they can take up to three hours per week of paid time off for study, no matter where they are located. Once UTC workers graduate, there are no requirements placed on them to stay with the company or to repay education expenses; they can leave immediately if they are so inclined. The ESP is also available to laid-off employees, many of whom later return to the company for better-paying positions.

This is no small commitment. Through year-end 2015, UTC has invested over $1.18 billion in the program, yielding more than 37,000 degrees for employees in more than 50 participating countries. Adding in the time value of employees' paid leave to pursue their education, approximately 150 hours per employee per year, the total cost is obviously much higher.

When asked about this expense, CEO George David (1994–2007), who initiated the program, would typically reply: "It's in our interest to have an educated workforce." But there was more to it than that. What UTC bought with that investment of more than a billion dollars was a jump in employee engagement and a surge in **relational equity** that quickly fed into shareholder equity.

From year-end 1997, the first full year ESP was in effect, until year-end 2015, UTC's stock grew more than five times in value and its annual dividend increased almost ninefold—a return that was nearly six times that of the S&P 500.

For a bottom-line-first company that manages by results (MBR), the costs of the scholarship program would have killed it. But, rather than focusing on cost, David took a more holistic approach called management by means (MBM). This approach recognizes that employees are the means by which companies achieve their results, that learning is the means by which employees grow their professional competence, and that the heart–brain connections of employees are the means to inspire their learning. From this perspective, the ESP was to be a multiplier—a proposition to take employees deeper into the ideals and values that give meaning to their work.

Looking back on the two decades since the ESP was introduced, it has supercharged a reinforcing cycle of living asset stewardship (LAS) leading to breakthrough green technologies in UTC's two core markets: the urban built environment and commercial aviation.

Like Ken Iverson's decision to make employees the central focus of Nucor's culture, George David's decision to offer employees open-ended college funding was a transformative leap of faith. In both instances, the goals were to **empower employees** by engaging their ideals, values, and intellects, and thereby transfer decision-making authority to the front lines where most operating knowledge resides.

But unlike Iverson, who took his transformative leap of faith from an intuitive sense of system, David's approach was more cerebral and attuned to systems thinking. Under his leadership, UTC became one of the first corporate members of the Society for Organizational Learning (SoL), a non-profit dedicated to systems thinking that emerged out of MIT in 1997, and in 1999 it became a founding member of SoL's Sustainability Consortium.

Bill Bucknall, UTC's senior vice president of human resources during the first 15 years of the ESP, was a key intellectual ally in its creation. As a graduate of MIT's Sloan School, which is closely affiliated with SoL, he appreciated the value of systems thinking and organizational learning and how these connected to innovation and profit.

We are a company of realists and optimists ... We invest authority where it needs to be, in the hands of the people closest to the customer and the work ... We seek and share ideas openly and encourage diversity of experience and opinion ... Our employees' ideas and inspiration create opportunities constantly, and without limits ... We support and pursue lifelong learning to expand our knowledge and capabilities and to engage with the world outside UTC.

UTC, "Our Commitments"[3]

Why UTC?

UTC is the focal point of this chapter because it shows how well the life-mimicking model works in a large industrial company— the very place we might expect to find ongoing applications of the industrial capitalist model.

What makes UTC doubly intriguing is the nature of its business units, which do not ordinarily excite investor enthusiasm. These include elevators (Otis), heating, ventilation and air conditioning (Carrier), jet engines (Pratt & Whitney), electrical power generation and distribution systems (Hamilton Sundstrand), and

---

3   UTC (2007). *Unwavering Commitment Continuous Improvement: 2007 Corporate Responsibility Report*, p. 3. Retrieved from http://www.socialfunds. com/shared/reports/1210167265_United_Technologies_2007_Corporate_ Responsibility_Report.pdf.

electronic security and fire safety systems (Chubb, Kidde)—hardly stuff that conjure images of life.

The magic, as we will see, is how George David united these industrial divisions into a coherent whole by:

- Giving them a transcendent and cohesive sense of purpose

- Developing a company-wide flexible cell structure that continually enriches UTC with new learning and information

- Infusing those cells with a unified life-affirming DNA (operating system)

Implicit in this strategy was an understanding that living assets (people and Nature) are the primary sources of UTC's value creation. Consequently, from the time he became CEO, David worked to create a culture of LAS premised on respect and caring for employees, plus the health of the larger living systems in which UTC operates (society, biosphere).

Given the immense challenges of operating an engineering company that directly (via manufacturing) and indirectly (via customer use of its products), consumes vast amounts of resources and energy in a world of depleting resources and climate change, David knew that speed of learning was critical to UTC's survival. This, in turn, relied on the ability of all employees—not just those at the top—to see systems as a whole, to understand both the limits and the potentials of its global corporate ecosystem.

As mentioned earlier, David did this by promoting a culture in which the means of achieving UTC's goals were congruent with the goals themselves. Although it took the better part of a decade to develop the emotional infrastructure, he succeeded by consistently modeling the attributes of leadership he wanted to infuse at every level: the qualities of respectful listening and the openness to disruptive ideas that exist in all transformative learning environments.

To further the spirit of exploration and experimentation, David encouraged UTC business units to become learning labs imbued with life-mimicking lean manufacturing techniques modeled on those pioneered at Toyota and Matsushita—a story we will return to later. As new learning emerged from these labs, the knowledge gained spread quickly through the company. The outcome was a homegrown process of continuous improvement that employees trusted because, having helped develop it from the ground up, they knew its effectiveness.

The success of this integrative, holistic management approach is reflected in UTC's reduced ecological footprint and care for employees, which have generated a reinforcing loop of lower costs and employee engagement. Reflecting this, operating margins more than doubled from roughly 6% in the mid-1990s, when David became CEO, to 15% in 2015.

We find evidence of this in UTC's 2015 annual report, which cites absolute reductions over the prior decade of greenhouse gas emissions (32%), industrial process waste (43%), water use (37%), and other emissions (65%), resulting in cost savings of more than $100 million. During the same period UTC reported 63% fewer lost workdays, which also reduced its costs of healthcare and employee absenteeism.

Helpful as these cost savings are, however, the larger benefit to UTC's operating margins derives from the enthusiasm employees feel about the work they do.

Meaningful work

UTC's 2006 corporate responsibility report presented employees with a galvanizing thought: that "UTC grows at the intersection of human progress and human concern."[4] In those few words it acknowledged their desires to work for a higher purpose than money alone and reinforced its mission to become a global leader in reversing climate change.

That mission, as mentioned earlier, is focused on two powerful megatrends, urbanization and the rapid growth in commercial aviation—areas that consume vast amounts of energy and increasingly scarce Earth resources. As noted by the Pew Center on Global Climate Change, the unifying theme of this is "one company constantly finding new technologies that make cities more efficient, people more secure and travel more comfortable [based on] the conversion of energy into useful work."[5]

By committing to reduce humanity's ecological footprint in both areas, UTC's employees thus had a clear context of work that had meaning to them and their families. Adding to their interest, UTC's leaders often describe the company's work in ways that instill pride and commitment.

Consider, for example, a 2012 address by Louis Chênevert, George David's successor as CEO, in which he described UTC's green technology challenge in heroic terms:

> [W]e innovate in an environment where failure is not an option. We're also not a "million new products a year" type of industry. Rather, our products are developed over decades, and they are highly complex—far more complex than the products

---

4   UTC (2006). *2006 Corporate Responsibility Report*, p. 1. Retrieved from https://ddd.uab.cat/pub/infsos/47169/irsUTCa2006ieng.pdf.

5   William R. Prindle (2010). *From Shop Floor to Top Floor: Best Business Practices in Energy Efficiency*. Arlington, VA: Pew Center on Global Climate Change, p. 85. Retrieved from http://www.c2es.org/docUploads/PEW_EnergyEfficiency_UTC.pdf.

many people consider innovative, such as smart phones and tablet computers.[6]

Speaking a few months later, Geraud Darnis, CEO of UTC's Building and Industrial Systems Division, gave further impetus to this theme. Speaking to a global engineering conference, he envisioned a time when buildings will "leapfrog the zero impact stage" and positively contribute to the environment:

> Instead of consuming power, buildings will supply power. Instead of shedding water, buildings will manage and filter rainwater back to the water table. Buildings will be ecosystems themselves and rest in balance with the natural environment. They will evolve from a drain on our resources, to a regeneration of our resources.[7]

The following year, Michael Winter, Chief Engineer for Technology at UTC's Pratt & Whitney division, commenting on revolutionary advances made by Pratt & Whitney's PurePower® jet engines, imagined future gains in aircraft engine efficiencies that would approach carbon neutrality.[8]

Given UTC's technology prowess, these visionary statements were not idle boasts for they are regularly supported by tangible results. At the time of Winter's talk, for example, planes equipped with UTC's revolutionary PurePower® PW1000G engine had already achieved 16–20% reductions in fuel use and greenhouse gas

6   Louis Chênevert (2012). Comments to a Wings Club luncheon, New York City, January 19, 2012. Retrieved from https://www.wingsclub.org/photos/speeches/louis-chenevert-2012-january-luncheon.

7   Geraud Darnis (2012). *The Future in Focus*, p. 3. Retrieved from http://www.utc.com/News/News-Center/Documents/2012-03-19_darnis.pdf.

8   Michael Winter (2013). *A View into the Next Generation of Commercial Aviation (2025 Timeframe)*. Retrieved from https://www.aiaa.org/uploadedFiles/Events/Other/Corporate/2013_-_Aerospace_Todayand_Tomorrow/Winter.pdf.

emissions relative to competitive models, plus 50% lower air pollutant emissions and 75% noise reductions. Because of this, planes such as the Airbus 340 reduced their carbon emissions by 3,000–3,600 metric tons per year while achieving savings on fuel and maintenance averaged roughly $1.5 million per year.

> Not since the arrival of the Boeing 747 in 1970 had there been serious innovation in jet engines.
>
> *Time* magazine[9]

A key part of George David's brilliance, and that of his leadership team, was acknowledging that such technology breakthroughs are rarely the work of a single individual or leadership team. Rather, they are the result of collaborative efforts that develop over time by engaging all the intellectual resources of every employee from the front lines up.

One of the most important factors in developing such collaboration is a spirit of **servant leadership,** where the role of leaders at every level is to serve the growth of employees through feedback, mentoring, cross-training, and thoughtful listening. This is especially important at times when work teams make mistakes or have to adjust to unexpected surprises—events that test their resolve, learning capacities, and creativity.

An excellent example of servant leadership at work is the way in which employees at a Pratt & Whitney plant scheduled for closure in 1992 reinvented its operating systems in such a way that the plant gained a new lease of life and became a world-renowned center of

9   Bill Saporito (2011, May 19). How to build a job engine. *Time*. Retrieved from http://content.time.com/time/magazine/article/0,9171,2072633-2,00.html.

productivity. This story is now legend at UTC because it inspired changes in the whole company's operating system and symbolized the can-do spirit of inspired employees.

A company that learns from itself

The plant in question was located in North Berwick, Maine. When its manager got notice he had six months to wind down the operation, he took matters into his own hands. Over the course of a weekend he and some key employees rearranged a major section of the plant from a production line into a "flexible cell" structure.

In this single stroke, he made UTC's networked organization more lifelike by replicating the self-making, self-regenerating, and self-organizing cell structure of a living organism. Just as cells transmit energy and information within the human body, they would do so at North Berwick and ultimately to the entire company.

The plant at the time of its radical conversion was already a corporate learning lab that was experimenting with Japanese lean manufacturing techniques. So what the manager and his team did was consistent with ongoing practices.

To shorten a long story, the North Berwick experiment was wildly successful. By rearranging employees into self-organizing cells of 5–10 people and teaching them how to make process improvements on their own, the plant gained a new lease of life.

To assist employees in learning these new methods, the plant manager created a change team of teachers in flexible manufacturing, quality control, and reducing process waste. Guided by such coaching, employees in each cell became more interested in their work. More importantly, as their operating knowledge grew, they began to share insights and ideas, with the best ones passed along to other cells. By building on such feedbacks, the plant quickly became a world-class productivity exemplar, attracting hundreds of visitors each year.

According to a definitive MIT study, over the four-year period from its turnaround to 1996, the North Berwick plant increased its revenues by a factor of five while also reducing by 25% the number of square feet needed for operations.[10]

Moved by its rapid improvements in productivity and quality, Pratt & Whitney leaders renewed the plant's operating status and began testing it as a model for the entire division. Based on the success of those tests, the new system was rolled out in 1996 with all divisional departments reorganized into flexible cells modeled on those at North Berwick.

To give the new system an air of panache, team members called it ACE—an acronym for Achieve Competitive Excellence. The name, which conjured an image of star aircraft pilots, caught on quickly. Experts in the new cellular system became known as ACE pilots. Their role was to lead further changes throughout Pratt & Whitney, which by then had become a learning lab for the whole company.

Inspired by the 1996 Olympic games in Atlanta, cells and sites that met UTC's high standards of technical skill, operational improvement, employee satisfaction, safety, quality, and financial success were recognized by certifications of bronze, silver, or gold. Like the ACE name itself, these designations became part of an information and energy feedback loop that encouraged productivity while giving employees a sense of pride and esprit.

10   George L. Roth (2010). *United Technologies Corporation: Achieving Corporate Excellence (ACE)—an Operating System Case Study*, pp. 21 and 23. Retrieved from https://dspace.mit.edu/handle/1721.1/81998.

Impressed by the North Berwick experience and the enthusiasm of Pratt & Whitney employees for the new system, George David, in collaboration with UTC division vice presidents, decided in 1997 to institutionalize the lessons learned by creating the new position of Corporate Vice President of Quality. From this point on, the organic flexible cell structure became an integral part of UTC's culture.

The amazing part of this story is how quickly and competently the lessons learned at the North Berwick plant were adopted at the divisional and then corporate level. Given its flexibility, at each step along the way, process improvements were made. It was as if a new strain of DNA had entered the system, speeding up UTC's capacities to learn and adapt.

ACE as a cultural paradigm

To fully appreciate the evolution of ACE within UTC and the provenance of its cultural DNA, it is important to recognize the influence of Yuzuru Ito, whom George David regarded "as a father." The two met in 1986 while David, then President of UTC's Otis division, was trying to solve a quality problem with Nippon Otis elevators at Matsushita Electric's new corporate headquarters in Osaka, Japan. Because Nippon Otis was a joint venture of the two companies, the elevator problem was both an embarrassment and a blow to Matsushita's reputation.

Given the gravity of the problem, David asked Ito, who was Quality Vice President of Matsushita, for help and advice. What he learned during this exercise later became a core element of the flexible cell system and ultimately the ACE program.

Ito-san taught Nippon Otis employees new statistical diagnostic techniques and how to create self-organizing quality clinics—essentially giving them the knowledge and confidence to spot and solve quality problems on their own. With these new self-managing processes at their disposal, the volume and quality of employee production increased dramatically. This both solved the proximate elevator problem and transformed David's management thinking.

From that time forward Ito and David were in continuous contact. When Ito retired from Matsushita in 1991, he continued consulting with Otis. When David was later promoted to CEO of UTC in 1994, one of his first acts was to hire Ito as an in-house teacher. Several years later, when David introduced ACE as UTC's operating system, the program he created to carry it forward was dubbed Ito University.

David's respect for Ito's teaching was part of an ongoing fascination with *kaizen*, a collaborative practice based on respectful listening, where all parties interested in a problem come together, first to deconstruct the problem (*kai*), then to imagine ways to improve the situation to everyone's benefit (*zen*).

One of Ito's core principles was to treat any malfunction on the plant floor as a learning opportunity, subject to "problem-solving," rather than finding someone to blame. He also taught that the best way to improve working conditions in a plant was to leverage the natural curiosity and desire of employees to innovate together. A true servant leadership style, it focused on relationships, respectful listening, and thoughtful collaboration—the very essence of MBM. More poignantly, it emphasized the value of the human heart.

> The human heart is considered to be the most important thing in any management method. Learning a management tool is easy in some sense. However, ... [i]f activities of the human hearts are neglected, any tool can be no longer effective. Managers need to spend more efforts to study human hearts frankly than to study management tools.
>
> Yuzuru Ito[11]

Reflecting these ideals, one of the most important features of the ACE process is the give and take of dialogue in what came to be known as "Leadership and followership for continuous improvement." Conceived as a means of organizational learning, it is a deferential practice of asking questions, listening to ideas, and brainstorming, where the leaders in a discussion are those with the most penetrating questions or pertinent information, regardless of rank.

Now modeled at every level of the firm, the leadership/followership method was embedded in the very creation of the ACE operating system itself. Before formally launching the program, George David spent two years listening to ideas, objections, and feedback from UTC's divisional heads.

As these practices developed within UTC, knowledge and ideas held by individuals and groups came forward more quickly. During "kaizen events," teams engaged in intense analysis of workplace

---

11 Ito Quality Philosophy, from UTC internal web site, dated as written by Yuzuru Ito in September 1998, quoted in George L. Roth (2010). *United Technologies Corporation: Achieving Corporate Excellence (ACE)—an Operating System Case Study*, p. 19. Retrieved from https://dspace.mit.edu/handle/1721.1/81998.

conditions with a focus on how to create more value with less capital expense, less employee stress, and reduced inventories. By concentrating on intellectual value added by employees, rather than capital-intensive economies of scale, work teams gained a sense of pride and control over their work.

Commenting on this method nearly a decade after the ACE program was initiated, David said:

> Every time we do a lean [*kaizen*] event in a plant, and this is broadly true, we double capacity and halve cost. That is why we built the last bricks and mortar in UTC years ago. ... You don't need [high investment rates] in a knowledge based company like ours, where manufacturing productivity is at super high levels.[12]

The effectiveness of these MBM practices is affirmed when we compare shareholder returns on UTC stock relative to those of General Electric, a leading proponent of MBR. Between year-end 1997—the year ACE was introduced—through 2015, UTC's shares grew more than fourfold while those of General Electric were virtually unchanged.

ACE as operating system

Since the early days, when ACE was rolled out from UTC's Pratt & Whitney division to the whole company, it has been revised and refreshed many times. From this perspective, it is a *living* system that adapts and evolves over time, rather than a fixed set of rules that rarely change.

---

12   Quoted in George L. Roth (2010). *United Technologies Corporation: Achieving Corporate Excellence (ACE)—an Operating System Case Study*, p. 4. Retrieved from https://dspace.mit.edu/handle/1721.1/81998.

In its earliest (1996) iterations, ACE was primarily focused on manufacturing plant operations. While this led to new insights and efficiencies, it often caused managers to focus so much on the micro (cellular) level that they lost touch with the macro system in which UTC operates—a system that includes diverse stakeholders (customers, suppliers, investors, host communities) plus the environment. To correct that deficiency an ACE Council, consisting of divisional ACE managers, was created in 2001.

The council's purpose was to transcend divisional and business unit boundaries to create a unified system that could be used by all. By being broadly inclusive in its deliberations, it became a forum where ACE could develop organically from the bottom up. Everyone's insights and opinions mattered. The aim was to improve performance along UTC's entire value stream by bringing every site up to the same high (gold and silver) levels.

The important quality of these exchanges was the council's willingness to listen and adapt rather than dictate. Over time, these collegial exchanges led to important new methods of making ACE more holistic and accretive, including:

- Broadening ACE from its focus on quality-driven manufacturing cells to broader business applications through "value stream mapping"

- Bringing suppliers into the ACE operating system, with clear performance goals and expectations

- Placing more emphasis on the means of capacity building (MBM) by focusing on employee morale, ethics, honest communication, and "the Spirit of ACE"

- Developing balanced scorecard metrics that look to employee engagement, customer satisfaction, and other forms of relational equity

- Creating transparent ACE dashboards for each site that give continuous feedback on business performance

- Incorporating ACE performance into everyone's bonus pay

- Teaching employees at all levels through ACE specialists and UTC's in-house Ito University to ensure that everyone is on board with new developments

One of the most important unifying features of the ACE system is the ubiquity of ACE boards at all UTC plants. Like the human central nervous system, these provide continuous feedback on the health and vitality of each systemic part in terms of its organization, goals, the status of its work, continuous improvement projects, and results.

ACE Assessors (formerly ACE pilots) perform additional feedback as in-house learning consultants. Together with the ACE boards they comprise a double-loop learning system that evaluates workplace performance (the first loop) plus working assumptions that may affect that performance (the second loop). This advanced learning process allows UTC to learn organically from experience as it moves ahead, rather than mechanistically using the same thought processes over and over again as if the world operated on a fixed set of mechanistic laws.

This approach to learning is another common feature of companies that mimic life because it engages employees in reflection: evaluating why things happen rather than simply measuring what happened. This ability to see systems in a more holistic context is critical to a team's understanding and vision and, by extension, to their speed of learning and adaptation.

While the primary strength of the ACE operating system is its breadth and depth of vision, the system would not work without a shared neurology and cultural DNA.

Maintaining that neurological wiring is primarily the responsibility of the President's Council (a group composed of the CEO, CFO, division presidents, and other key leaders). The ACE Council (made up of managers from each division) is more concerned with cultural variables, which include employee morale, customer satisfaction, and speed of learning.

A nonlinear feedback system

The importance of these councils, like those of the ACE boards at work sites, is to continually weigh feedback from diverse sources within UTC's business ecosystem. The diversity, complexity, and forward-looking nature of these feedbacks provide an evolving image of the firm's relational equity.

Qualitatively, the strength of these feedbacks resides in their nonlinearity: their ability to see systems as a whole rather than just the parts that have a more direct bearing on bottom line results. This gives UTC an ability to anticipate change ahead of competitors.

As summarized on UTC's website: "ACE has three elements: culture, tools and competency. The daily interaction of each element is what makes it an operating system. Results focus on perfect quality, on-time delivery, highly engaged employees working in a safe environment, and best-in-class financial returns."[13]

Culture is important because it affects the ease with which information flows through the system via UTC's diverse stakeholders (employees, suppliers, customers, governments, etc.). Tools, such as key performance indicators (KPIs), measure current performance and forward-looking metrics, including employee wellbeing and

13   UTC (2016). Our operating system. Retrieved from http://www.utc.com/Our-Company/Our-Operating-System/Pages/default.aspx.

customer satisfaction. Competence relates to the dedication of the men and women who serve in flexible operating cells and other teams as measured by UTC's gold, silver, and bronze operating performance designations.

In order to promote better understanding of the relationships between KPIs and variables such as market penetration and profitability, data on both financial and nonfinancial results is today disclosed in "integrated" annual financial reports—a practice initiated in 2008 by then Chief Financial Officer Gregory Hayes.[14]

According to the Harvard Business School professors, Robert G. Eccles and George Serafeim, UTC was the first U.S. company to adopt such reporting, which is today considered a transparency best practice. They describe how the diversity of information provided in integrated reports creates "holistic" feedback loops that provide a "transformation function"—enabling companies to engage in "conversations that otherwise would not occur, insights that would not otherwise surface, and innovations that would not otherwise materialize," resulting in a more efficient and productive allocation of capital.[15]

UTC's approach relies on a company-wide, mandatory reporting system for energy use and costs. Every manufacturing site as well as any site with more than $100,000 in annual energy and water costs must report quarterly through the online, enterprise-level data system. For UTC, this puts

14   Hayes subsequently became CEO at year-end 2014 on the retirement of Louis Chênevert.
15   Robert G. Eccles & George Serafeim (2014). Corporate and integrated reporting: a functional perspective. Retrieved from http://ssrn.com/abstract=2388716.

> data from some 300 facilities into the system. ...
> Site managers must input data quarterly, which
> get rolled up into EH&S reports summarized at
> the business unit level that go to senior manage-
> ment.
>
> Pew Center on Global Climate Change[16]

MBM as an emerging concept

Like the ACE operating system, the concept of MBM is relatively new. First articulated in 2000 by Tom Johnson and Anders Broms in their classic *Profit Beyond Measure*,[17] it has coevolved with corporate trends toward networking and biomimicry and is today a core feature of all companies that competently mimic life.

Modeled on the Toyota Production System, with its emphasis on collaborative learning and *kaizen*, MBM reveals the power of caring, holistic thinking, and engaging the hearts of employees in their work.

LAS is the emotional and spiritual infrastructure that underpins MBM because it holds corporate (and all human) networks together. By giving weight to an organization's impacts on Nature and society, LAS touches our life-affirming biophilic instincts, which unite all humanity—inspiring us to learn as we seek meaning in what we do. The genius of life-mimicking companies such as UTC

---

16 William R. Prindle (2010). *From Shop Floor to Top Floor: Best Business Practices in Energy Efficiency*. Arlington, VA: Pew Center on Global Climate Change, p. 92. Retrieved from http://www.c2es.org/docUploads/PEW_EnergyEfficiency_UTC.pdf.

17 H. Thomas Johnson & Anders Broms (2000). *Profit Beyond Measure: Extraordinary Results Through Attention to Work and People*. New York, NY: The Free Press.

resides in knowing how to activate these instincts and channel them into productive learning.

To socio-biologist Edward O. Wilson, who coined the term "biophilia," the human quest for meaning impels us toward "unified learning"—a synthesis of knowledge from the sciences and humanities that transcends the intellectual boundaries of specialization. At the center of it is an ecological awakening that humanity is one of millions of interdependent species on Earth, and that we need the biodiversity of functioning ecosystems to sustain our lives and those of future generations.

We are entering a new era of existentialism [based on] the concept that only unified learning, universally shared, makes accurate foresight and wise choice possible. In the course of it all, we are learning that ethics is everything.

Edward O. Wilson, Consilience[18]

While this may sound esoteric in relation to the standard operating procedures of industrial capitalism, it is lodged in the very heart of the employee scholar and ACE programs, which have catalyzed UTC's success.

From this perspective, the operating leverage of MBM resides in the things that matter most to us as people: our instinctive desires to live and work in harmony with Nature and society, and our thirst for new knowledge and insights to make this happen. After all, the one thing that most closely binds us to all life on Earth is the will to pass our genes on to another generation.

---

18   Edward O. Wilson (1998). *Consilience: The Unity of Knowledge*. New York, NY: Alfred A. Knopf, p. 297.

4

Conservation of resources

The most important change in recent times has been the enormous growth of one subsystem of the Earth, namely the economy, relative to the total system, the ecosphere ... The closer the economy approaches the scale of the whole Earth the more it will have to conform to the physical behavior mode of the Earth.

Herman E. Daly[1]

[T]he majority of our future electricity supplies will be generated from wind.

Novo Nordisk Annual Report, 2008[2]

1   Herman E. Daly (2008). A steady-state economy. Retrieved from http://www.sd-commission.org.uk/data/files/publications/Herman_Daly_thinkpiece.pdf.
2   Novo Nordisk (2008). *Novo Nordisk Annual Report 2008,* p. 3. Retrieved from http://www.novonordisk.co.uk/content/dam/Denmark/HQ/Commons/documents/Novo_Nordisk_UK_AR2008.pdf.

Sustainability and profitability have long gone hand in hand at Novo Nordisk (a Danish manufacturer of the pharmaceutical, insulin). This was particularly evident during the global economic recession of 2008–2009. While other companies deferred or slowed environmental spending, believing it to be marginally productive at best, Novo took aggressive measures to lower its ecological footprint by switching its Danish operations to green electric power and reprocessing waste-water for reuse. Barely reflecting these and other capital expenses related to energy and water, the net income of Novo's global operations increased more than 27% during that two-year period. This enabled it to add nearly $1.1 billion to cash reserves, which raised the year-end 2009 net cash surplus on its balance sheet to $2.2 billion.

The story of Novo's switch to green energy during this period speaks volumes about the company's culture. Starting in 2006, after a campaign to increase employees' awareness of climate change, the management challenged Danish work teams to reduce energy waste as a first step toward converting its home operations to renewable energy. The following year Novo signed a partnership agreement with DONG Energy, its Danish electricity supplier, pledging to use Novo's domestic energy savings to purchase renewable energy certificates for a planned new North Sea wind farm.

Employees took up the challenge with gusto. As revealed in its 2008 annual report, half their suggested energy saving schemes had payback times of less than a year while "a quarter ... required no upfront investment, only changes in facility management."[3] The end result was a cost-neutral way to achieve significant reductions in CO_2 emissions while simultaneously helping to build the market for renewable energy in Denmark.

3   Ibid., p. 28.

Such dedication and engagement is hard to imagine in bottom-line-first companies that manage by results (MBR). But it came naturally at Novo because everyone felt a personal stake in the matter: both as concerned electricity-consuming citizens and as involved corporate stakeholders.[4]

Novo's capacity to generate record profits while making large capital investments—accomplished during a deep global recession when most companies were cutting back—reflects the uplifting spirit of a firm that works to serve the whole ecosystem in which it operates rather than the single goal of profit. As such, it is a compelling example of the operating leverage companies achieve when their practices of living asset stewardship (LAS) deepen and spread.

While Novo has been a progressive company since its founding in 1923, it deepened its efforts to become more eco-effective on its 50th birthday in 1973. At that time it was a minor player in the pharmaceutical industry, then dominated by Merck, Pfizer, Lilly, and other global giants. However, in the ensuing decades to 2015 it rapidly caught up. By inspiring employees to think in a resource-conserving holistic context, it became the clear sector leader in both industrial ecology and profit.

Novo's leadership in these areas is affirmed by the spectacular growth of its common stock. From the turn of the century to year-end 2015, its share price grew in value 25-fold while its cash dividend increased 38-fold from $0.025/share to $0.96/share. By contrast, the share prices of Merck, Pfizer, and Lilly (its primary competitor in the global insulin market) all lost money. The share price of Sanofi, another insulin manufacturer, showed modest gains during this period, but nothing remotely close to Novo.

---

4   With four employee representatives on Novo's 11-member board, community voices are prominently heard.

Novo's competitive edge

Novo's competitive edge over these pharma giants resides in its inspiring culture, where respect for life—here defined as working in harmony with Nature and society—is a universal corporate value. Because this culture is supported by robust metric systems, ubiquitous transparency, and employee participation, it has become virtually self-perpetuating.

Eco-intensity ratios (EIRs) measure energy and water consumption at every level of production, including that of key suppliers. Overseen by a team of global "energy stewards," EIR targets are refreshed every year on an annual and long-term basis to ensure continual improvement with a goal of reducing Novo's ecological footprint even as production volume grows.

Novo's EIRs are part of a larger integrated system of environmental profit and loss (EPL) accounts. By converting environmental metrics, such as water use in cubic feet or carbon emissions in tons, into monetary terms, Novo puts its environmental impacts on an equal footing with more traditional business/financial concerns. Looking beyond its own impacts, EPL statements also encompass its supply chain. Further, system-wide results are a consideration in CEO compensation.

In common with these environmental policies and practices, Novo further expresses its respect for life through clear, high standards on bioethics and human rights. With more than 80 employees dedicated to addressing bioethical dilemmas and supervising the company's handling of bioethical issues worldwide, Novo's bioethical monitoring covers research involving people, animals, human materials and gene technology.[5] The same standards apply to external contractors, who are selected based on their ethical track records. Few companies anywhere come close to these standards.

In the area of human rights, Novo is likewise far ahead of its corporate peers. In 1998, it was one of the first companies to sign the Universal Declaration of Human Rights. Today its "Global Labor Guidelines" adhere to the highest standards of the United Nations (UN) Global Compact. Similarly, these standards also apply to external contractors, which are regularly monitored.

Collectively, these progressive policies look to a "triple bottom line" of ecological, social, and economic returns—a generative concept based on symbiotic feedbacks. In theory and practice it works like this: healthy people and healthy planet support healthy business; healthy business, in turn, supports healthy people and planet by reinvesting profits in life-supporting ways. The interplay of such mutual interests replicates the circular processes of Nature that have operated since life on Earth began 3.5 billion years ago.

Novo's dedication to triple bottom line strategies is elegantly expressed in its "Blueprint for Change": a public–private partnership dedicated to reducing and containing diabetes, the world's fastest-growing public health epidemic. Conceived as a global program, Novo approaches each market by framing its unique diabetes-related challenges together with leverage points where early intervention can save lives, reduce social overhead costs, and improve economic performance. Working with local governments, NGOs, and health organizations, it then creates strategies to optimize those leverage points.

---

5   Novo Nordisk (2008). *Animals in Pharmaceutical Research and Development: Bioethics in Action.* Retrieved from https://www.novonordisk.com/ content/dam/Denmark/HQ/RND/Documents/Bioethics_Animals%20 UK_25-09.pdf.

The effectiveness of such strategies is clear. By pursuing the triple bottom line in an authentic, disciplined way, Novo achieves a multiple win: increasing demand for its products, lowering its costs of production (via the EIRs), and inspiring employees in ways that have made it the world's innovation leader in diabetes care.

> Health is a driver of wealth. It is a basic human right, yet, for many, remains something that must be fought for. In a sustainable scenario this will no longer be necessary—access to basic healthcare must be a minimum requirement and professional care should be available in any community.
> Lars R. Sørensen, President and CEO, Novo Nordisk[6]

The depth and authenticity of Novo's approach is further expressed by its policy on tax payments, which affect the welfare of the countries where it operates. Rather than booking sales and profits from tax havens as most of its industry peers do—a practice known as "transfer pricing"—Novo pays taxes directly to the countries where profits are earned. In 2015, it paid an average effective worldwide rate of 19.8% while its Big Pharma peers, such as Pfizer (regularly named as one of America's top tax avoiders), paid little or no tax.

The takeaway point here is that Novo's holistic, conservation-minded strategy produces better financial, environmental, and social returns than its conventionally managed peers—in spite of

6   Novo Nordisk (2013). *United Nations Global Compact Communication on Progress 2013*, p. 2. Retrieved from http://www.novonordisk.com/content/dam/Denmark/HQ/Sustainability/documents/novo-nordisk-communication-on-progress-2013.pdf.

paying higher taxes. While hard-nosed corporate leaders may dismiss Novo's green energy, bioethics, human rights, and transparency practices as soft or extreme, they can only look with envy at its results.

From triple top line to bottom line

As an ideal, the triple bottom line is premised on the reality that profit can only emerge from life, in which case sustainable companies must use profit to serve life. The key word here is "serve," and it conveys a spectrum of meanings: from giving something back to society and biosphere (at a minimum) to being ecologically regenerative.

The ideal of being regenerative is top-line. It aligns means and ends in ways that traditional bottom-line thinking never can because it starts at the beginning of Novo's value-creating processes. This gives the company an authenticity and coherence from start to finish. It also inspires employees to become engaged, and to transform shared life-affirming ideals into meaningful innovation.

Novo's integrated annual report—which explores the linkages between financial, environmental, and social results—is an important statement of its regenerative intentions because it shows employees and other stakeholders how top and bottom line are connected. In recognition of this clarity, CorporateRegister.com has designated Novo's annual report as the "world's Best Integrated Report" five times out of seven (most recently in April 2013).

To further embed top-line ideals into its culture, Novo invites diverse NGOs to visit its facilities and offer constructive feedback on improving its social and ecological performance. Since 2003, it has also run an employee engagement program—called

"TakeAction!"—that offers young professionals volunteer activities on matters that have personal meaning to them, ranging from diabetes care to ecological issues. Coordinated with various NGOs, including the World Wildlife Fund (WWF), this program gives employees an opportunity to get real-world, problem-solving experience with fellow team members. By so honoring and affirming the values of staff, Novo secures their allegiance and dedication to join in the quest for top-line solutions.

This high level of employee engagement correlates strongly with Novo's returns on assets and equity. As reflected in Table 4.1, these returns are significantly higher than its pharmaceutical industry peers for the five-year period ending in December 2015—in spite of the fact that Novo uses less debt leverage to achieve them.

The essential point here is that Novo doesn't need the mechanistic leverage of borrowing because top-line means and bottom-line ends are in synch. Inspired, well-informed employees—people who work with their hearts as well as their minds—are more productive than those who simply follow orders.

It is worth bearing these distinctions in mind when evaluating traditionally managed companies that profess to have triple bottom line cultures (as do Lilly, Merck, Pfizer, and Sanofi). Because such

TABLE 4.1 Comparative results at year-end 2015

Company	Five-year average returns (%)		Total debt/ equity ratio
	On assets	On equity	
Novo Nordisk	34.8	61.0	2.4
Lilly	10.4	24.4	45.2
Merck	6.4	13.1	44.9
Pfizer	5.1	11.8	50.6
Sanofi	4.8	8.2	26.7

Source: http://www.factset.com

firms are more focused on linear cost accounting principles and MBR directives, their methods too often conflict with their professed life-affirming goals of realigning their (nonlinear) relationships with humanity and Nature.

Had Novo Nordisk taken the narrow linear accounting approach, it would never have converted its Danish operations to wind energy because the least-cost option was in fossil fuels. But Novo saw past that to the enthusiasm employees felt about its larger goals of living and working in harmony with Nature, which is the true (biophilic) source of their engagement and creativity.

From net positive impact to high-order learning

The inspirational goal of Novo's regenerative agenda is to move beyond zero environmental impact to "net positive impact." This strongly resonates with employees and rouses their high-order spiritual intelligence, which so powerfully directs IQ and the desire to learn.

This dynamic is accentuated by traditions that promote double-loop learning. For example, employees are encouraged to question (and test) their methods and assumptions as they test incoming data. From the lab to the plant floor, everything is up for discussion including difficult subjects, such as gene technology and animal testing. This ensures that new information is scrutinized for potentially valuable new insights rather than accepted at face value.

While these practices deepen Novo's capacity for learning and insight, the company broadens its perspective by engaging the minds of its 40,000 employees in advancing its life-affirming mission. This gives it a capacity to gather and process far more information than a top-down hierarchy ever could.

Say what you will about the complexities of open, democratic workplaces, Novo's capacity to produce industry-leading profits by respectfully listening to its employees has worked brilliantly.

If you want to create holistic collaborations where team members become systems within a system, allowing them to become creative and emergent at every level, then you've got to act from the higher motivations.

Danah Zohar[7]

One of the best examples of Novo's learning culture at work is its leadership in industrial ecology. Inspired by visions of creating more value with fewer virgin resources and lower adverse impacts on Nature, its employees have for decades found creative ways to lower operating costs and generate extra revenue.

Toward industrial ecology

Long before the concept of industrial ecology (IE) became popularized via a *Scientific American* article,[8] Novo practiced IE at its largest plant in Kalundborg, Denmark. The working premise at that time (early 1970s) was to use the wastes from one industrial process

---

7   Danah Zohar (2004). A new capitalism we can live by: an interview with Danah Zohar. *Leverage Points*, 54.

8   R.A. Frosch & N.E. Gallopoulos (1989). Strategies for manufacturing. *Scientific American*, 261(3), 144-152.

as raw materials for another, thereby reducing the impact of local industries on the environment.

Over succeeding decades, as IE practices at Kalundborg became more fastidious, the region evolved into a highly integrated "industrial symbiosis" (a subject we shall pick up in Chapter 8). Significantly, Novo was a key leader in all these developments.

As a resource management discipline, IE today combines perspectives of traditional sciences, such as biology, chemistry, and physics, with those of the humanities, such as economics, psychology, and sociology. In doing so, it brings human enterprise into closer accord with Nature through processes of product design (ecodesign) and assessing the impacts of products through their life-cycles.

The ideal of IE is to **replicate the metabolic functions of living systems** by following the flows of materials and energy used in manufacturing through Nature and society: from resource extraction to ingestion (production), digestion (product use), and ultimately death (product disposal), whereupon decay (wastage) becomes food for new resources (via recycling or reuse).

By such means, industrial ecology seeks to mitigate adverse impacts early on through product design and life-cycle analysis rather than at "the end of the pipe" after considerable ecological damage has been done.

Novo's life-cycle analysis starts at the conceptual product development stage through a focus group called EnviroProcess, which operates under the aegis of its Environment, Bioethics and Health and Safety Committee. This group is primarily concerned with the environmental effects of energy, water, and chemicals used in production, plus waste and other emissions. It also studies the environmental impacts of postconsumer waste, such as the effects on aquatic ecosystems of estrogen-related hormone residues released into sewage and water systems. As described by senior research director Jesper Lau, the goal of this approach to new product and process development is to figure out how Nature works and to replicate it.[9]

Novo's cLEAN® program, introduced in 2003, mimics Nature by minimizing energy and material waste (entropy) in manufacturing. As a measure of its success, for the ten years ending in 2012, Novo more than doubled sales while making absolute reductions in its use of energy and water. Since then, in spite of adding substantial new manufacturing capacity in Brazil, China, Europe, and the U.S.A., it has committed to a bold company-wide target of zero carbon emissions by 2020—a goal it expects to meet by converting to renewable energy sources.

Beyond controlling its *direct* uses of energy and water in manufacturing, Novo has also committed to reducing its *indirect* uses via its supply chain, methods of product distribution, and employee travel. Equally important, it intends to transparently report on results so employees and other stakeholders can learn from its experience.

Novo's goal of running its Kalundborg insulin production with "renewable steam" is a cogent case in point. In collaboration with its process steam supplier (DONG Energy), it has set a goal to convert from coal to locally sourced biomass from 2019 onward.

Such collaboration on resource sharing and eco-efficiency has a long history at Novo. Since 1976, it has reprocessed wastes from the plant's fermentation tanks into fertilizer (NovoGro) for local crops and, since 1989, it has sold waste yeast slurry to pig farms as a feed supplement. In 2013, it joined its sister company, Novozymes, in producing biogas from waste-water with a reactor that "produces

9   Novo Nordisk (2014). Mimicking Mother Nature in the lab. *TBL Quarterly*, 4, 7-8 (p. 7). Retrieved from https://www.novonordisk.com/content/dam/Denmark/HQ/Sustainability/documents/TBL-Quarterly-no-4-2014.pdf.

as much electricity as 7 offshore wind turbines, reduces CO_2 emissions and lowers energy costs."[10]

Reflecting its multi-stakeholder approach in these ventures, the biogas generator is part of a larger collaboration called the BIOPRO Development Center: a venture that includes DONG Energy, Novozymes, the Danish Technical University, the University of Copenhagen, and a group of nearby biotech companies. The center's purpose is to keep investing ahead of the curve by reducing the use of virgin materials used in production while increasing product yields.

To further advance Novo's industrial ecology goals, the Novo Nordisk Foundation supports eco-inspired research at the BIOPRO World Talent Campus in Kalundborg. Open to PhD-level students from around the world, its program looks beyond Novo's needs to team-building activities that foster a global network of biotechnology manufacturing.

As Novo learns through such collaborations, and its own experience, it creates further positive impacts by engaging key suppliers in its quest for new knowledge. Augmented by a program of supplier audits, where both parties work to identify and redress inefficient practices, such collaborations have become a major factor in Novo's cost competitiveness.

While we'll continue to challenge ourselves and improve in the areas of energy and water consumption, waste reduction and direct carbon emissions, we're ready to broaden the scope of

---

10 Novozymes (2013, June 7). Novozymes utilizes wastewater to produce biogas. Retrieved from http://www.novozymes.com/en/news/news-archive/2013/06/novozymes-utilizes-wastewater-to-produce-biogas.

> our responsibility to include indirect CO_2 emissions. With overwhelming scientific evidence of the increased ... impact of climate change, we simply must set ourselves ambitious targets in this area.
>
> Jakob Riis, Executive Vice President
> and Chair, Social & Environmental
> Committee, Novo Nordisk [11]

With decades of experience to draw on, Novo's industrial ecology practices have become a prodigious win–win strategy. By mimicking Nature's circular processes of feedback and regeneration, and by infusing its culture with an ethical respect for life, it is at once a hothouse of learning and innovation and one of the world's most profitable companies.

The Novo Nordisk Way

The Novo Nordisk Way frames the firm's ethical credo. It states in a few words how Novo intends to live and work on this planet:

> We never compromise on quality and business ethics. ... We are open and honest, ambitious and accountable, and treat everyone with respect. We offer opportunities for our people to realise their potential.[12]

11   Novo Nordisk (2015). *Novo Nordisk Annual Report 2015*, p. 41. Retrieved from http://www.novonordisk.com/content/dam/Denmark/HQ/Commons/documents/Novo-Nordisk-Annual-Report-2015.PDF.

12   Novo Nordisk (2016). Novo Nordisk Way. Retrieved from http://www.novonordisk.com/about-novo-nordisk/novo-nordisk-way.html.

More importantly, it transcends the written word. Like the U.S. Declaration of Independence, its ideals inspire great thinking and invite employees to engage in ways that have emotional and spiritual value to them.

We find evidence of this in engagement surveys, where Novo's scores (86% in both 2014 and 2015) were far above the global average of 62% for large corporations—placing it solidly in the "best employer" category (based on Aon Hewitt surveys).

According to an Aon 2015 survey, companies that attain best employer scores generate 83% better shareholder returns than the global average[13]—a finding that is consistent (if understated) with Novo's results since the turn of the millennium.

Importantly, the provenance of Novo's high ethical standards dates back nearly a century to the founding of Novo and Nordisk in the early 1920s. This gives them an authenticity that is hard to replicate by creating high-sounding ideals at an executive retreat. An early example is the creation in 1924 of the Nordisk Insulin Foundation, which was established to ensure that part of the company's profit was given back to society to support scientific and humanitarian causes.

Adding to the authenticity of Novo's ethical culture, ethical issues are widely discussed at all levels, not just in committees that deal with sustainability issues. Novo's flat (nonhierarchical) structure and egalitarian mores encourage employees everywhere to be engaged in ethical dialogue, whenever they feel compelled.

To facilitate such dialogue, Novo openly discloses its impacts—both positive and negative—on Nature and society. It was, for example, the world's first company to issue an independently

13   Aon Hewitt (2015). *2015 Trends in Global Employee Engagement*, p. 1. Retrieved from http://www.aon.com/attachments/human-capital-consulting/2015-Trends-in-Global-Employee-Engagement-Report.pdf.

verified environment and bioethics report (1996) that included the use of animals and genetic engineering in its disclosure. In 2004, it was also the first to issue an "integrated" annual report on the financial and nonfinancial metrics used in pursuing its triple bottom line strategy. And in 2014, it further raised the bar by issuing an EPL report with quarterly updates; receiving in the same year a perfect score of 100 on bioethics from the Dow Jones Sustainability Index.

To assist employees and other stakeholders in looking more deeply into ethical issues, Novo today offers a website where they can get current information on topics of special interest. Included in this website are interactive games concerning the ethical challenges Novo faces in the areas of business ethics, climate change, economics, and health. The objective behind all these innovations is to invite people to think and share feedback that could take the company to the next level.

Bioethics is the term we use for all ethical issues related to the use of life science technologies for the discovery, development and production of pharmaceutical products. It is of utmost importance to Novo Nordisk, that we in the process of bringing a new product to the market, carefully consider the ethical implications of our research and development activities as well as being attentive to societal concerns.

"Bioethics at Novo Nordisk"[14]

---

14   Novo Nordisk (2016). Bioethics at Novo Nordisk. Retrieved from http://www.novonordisk.com/rnd/inside-r-d/bioethics/bioethics.html.

The "Blueprint for Change" strategy

Because the Novo Nordisk Way is a living set of principles, it continually evolves as the company becomes more advanced in its practice of LAS. One of the best examples of this is its "Blueprint for Change" strategy.

As mentioned earlier, the blueprint is a public–private partnership whose goal is to create "sustainable shared value" wherever Novo operates. With a focus on vulnerable, under-served people, the blueprint seeks to reduce national healthcare costs and enable people with diabetes to have longer productive lives through advocacy, philanthropy, strategic investing, and public engagement.

In keeping with its triple bottom line goal of service to society, Novo provides human insulin to 33 of the world's poorest countries at no more than 20% of the average price in the Western world. In collaboration with the Novo Nordisk Foundation, the Novo Nordisk Education Foundation, and the World Diabetes Foundation (which Novo cofounded), it also trains doctors and caregivers in developing countries, where diabetes often goes undiagnosed with dire consequences, including kidney failure, blindness, heart complications, and amputation.

In India, Novo also supports a global R&D center in Bangalore and licenses a local manufacturer (Torrent Pharmaceuticals) to produce its insulin therapies—practices it now replicates in other developing countries. This ethic of sharing its knowledge spreads best practices, making it a preferred partner wherever it operates.

The shared value in this strategy for Novo is twofold. First, as a direct result of its service to under-served markets, the blueprint expands world market share for its therapies. The second and arguably the larger benefit is indirect: the engagement of employees who want to make a difference and who believe Novo's triple bottom line approach is the best way to do it. The economic leverage of such engagement is evident in Novo's high returns on capital and investment relative to key competitors as shown in Table 4.1.

As a successful example to other companies, the blueprint will also have a multiplier effect. Success invites imitation. Those who learn from Novo's experience will have a better future than those who don't.

Ethical finance

As should be clear by now, ethics at Novo is indivisible. It underpins everything the company does including finance, a discipline where many firms that profess to have ethical cultures fall off the tracks. Nowhere is this better illustrated than its cautious approach to mergers and acquisitions (M&A).

Conventionally, M&A strategies are used as a means to achieve market domination, reduce overhead costs, and gain better control over pricing. They also appeal to CEOs as a justification for multi-million-dollar bonuses. From this perspective, such practices are too often about *quantities*, MBR, and ego gratification.

To Novo, whose ethical *qualities* support a culture of management by means (MBM), this is risky business. Consequently, when it makes the rare acquisition, it opts for smaller companies that fit with its culture—ones that can be quickly accretive without compromising its balance sheet.

The benefits of this cautious approach become apparent when we compare the integrity of Novo's assets and equity relative to those of its Big Pharma peers after making adjustments for accounting "goodwill" (a balance sheet adjustment that reflects the premium an acquiring company pays over the acquired company's book value).

As can be seen in Table 4.2, goodwill often comprises a large portion of the total reported assets and equity of Big Pharma firms. Should the corporate marriages facilitated by these premium prices fail to meet their economic objectives due to culture clash—an all-too-frequent outcome—the resulting dilution becomes a financial handicap and a credit risk. This goes a long way to explaining why the shares of Pfizer, Merck, and Lilly have lost value since the turn of the millennium and why those of Sanofi, since its hostile takeover of Aventis in August 2004, have failed to keep up with inflation.

The different approaches these companies take to M&A are clearly evident when we look at goodwill as a percentage of reported assets and shareholder equity. In Novo's case, there is no dilution. What you see is what you get. The other four, by contrast, having paid premium prices for assets that are presently under-performing,

TABLE 4.2 **Effect of goodwill on reported assets and equity (US$ million) at year-end 2015**

Variable	Novo	Pfizer	Merck	Sanofi	Lilly
Total reported assets	13,770	167,460	101,780	114,600	35,570
Less goodwill	0	48,240	17,720	43,900	4,040
Goodwill as % of total reported assets	0.00%	28.81%	17.40%	40.25%	8.80%
Shareholder equity	7,046	64,720	44,680	65,016	14,570
Less goodwill	0	48,240	17,720	43,900	4,040
Goodwill as % of shareholder equity	0.00%	74.54%	39.65%	67.52%	27.72%
Tangible assets (shareholder equity less goodwill)	7,046	16,480	26,690	21,116	10,530
Net debt	0	15,690	13,090	8,180	9,620
Net debt as % of tangible assets	0.00%	95.21%	49.04%	38.71%	91.36%

have a problem. This is especially visible when you look at goodwill as a percentage of shareholder equity, which ranges from 27.72% to 74.54%.

In particular, note the ratio of net debt to tangible assets, the bottom line of this table, because it is an often overlooked indicator of credit quality and corporate staying power. In Novo's case its tangible assets at year-end 2015 were unencumbered because it had roughly $3 billion more cash than debt. Pfizer's net debt, by contrast, represents more than 95% of its tangible assets because it had $15.69 billion more debt than cash—a result that correlates with its poor earnings results.

The point of looking at these disparities—beyond their obvious effects on balance sheet strength and shareholder performance—is to highlight the care Novo takes to protect its ethical culture. By conserving cash and being disciplined in its approach to M&A, it is better able to meet its ethical commitments to employees, customers, suppliers, and host communities.

Looking deeper into Novo's financial strategy, it also uses its net income and balance sheet strength to spread its ethical culture. Such was the case in 2000 when it split into three autonomous, ethics-driven firms: Novo Nordisk (the original pharmaceutical company), Novozymes (now the world leader in bio-innovation), and Novo A/S (the holding company and venture capital arm of the Novo Group). Described as a de-merger, this was, in fact, the very opposite of Big Pharma M&A trends.

Rather than diluting Novo's ethical DNA, the de-merger spread it further afield via Novo A/S, which is wholly owned by the Novo Nordisk Foundation. Because the foundation holds the A shares of both Novo Nordisk and Novozymes—from which it receives dividends plus the appreciated value of their shares—it had a substantial net equity of $6.3 billion at year-end 2013. According to its 2014 annual report, it used those resources to invest €683 million ($941

million) in Europe and North America in support of sustainable
ethical enterprise.[15]

> Throughout its history, social responsibility has
> been at the heart of the Novo Nordisk Foun-
> dation's activities. ... Through its support for
> research, the Foundation focuses on contribut-
> ing to sustainable development that can help
> solve some of the present global challenges while
> simultaneously addressing the needs of future
> generations.
>
> Novo Nordisk Foundation,
> *Facts and Results 2013*[16]

Considered in this context, Novo's ethics have a compounding
effect—one of intentionally spreading its cultural DNA. Conversely,
in companies where ethics is situational rather than foundational,
we find the opposite result of negligence, waste, corner-cutting,
and, too often, fraudulent behavior—behaviors that have greatly
harmed some of the world's largest pharmaceutical companies.

This very contrast is a major reason Novo was selected for this
chapter. By putting life ahead of capital and profits—in effect, by
conserving the resources that are most essential to its future—it has
done far better than its largest peers.

---

15 Novo Nordisk Foundation (2014). *Novo Nordisk Foundation Group: Facts
    and Results 2014*, p. 7. Retrieved from https://issuu.com/nnfoundation/docs/
    nnf_facts_2014.
16 Ibid., p. 15.

Managing in a resource-constrained world

Respect for life is fundamentally conserving because life is the source of all real value. When Novo stewards life—whether caring for people or stewarding Nature's biological resources—it conserves the sources of its future success.

Such stewardship is not just a source of competitive advantage, it is absolutely essential in today's resource-constrained world. Infinite consumption growth on a planet with finite resources is impossible. Companies that ignore this reality for the sake of short-term gain sentence themselves to certain failure—via takeover or death.

The core problem facing business today—more than the global debt overhang—is global ecological overshoot. Finances can be repaired, but depletion of the Earth's biological resources is a more difficult challenge because its insidious effects are long-lived (ecosystem collapse) or irreversible (species extinction).

According to the Global Footprint Network, humanity today extracts resources from the Earth 50–60% faster than they can be regenerated. Using moderate UN scenarios, by 2030 humanity will be using up the resources of two planet Earths.[17]

To be more specific, the WWF reports that, since 1970, the world's oceans and continents have lost half their vertebrate species (some scientists are calling this the Earth's "sixth great extinction"), and that, since 1960, a third of the world's arable land has been lost to the erosion caused by deforestation.[18] Looking to the future, the

17 Global Footprint Network (2016). World Footprint: do we fit on the planet? Retrieved from http://www.footprintnetwork.org/en/index.php/GFN/page/world_footprint/.

18 WWF (2014, September 30). Half of global wildlife lost, says new WWF report. Retrieved from http://www.worldwildlife.org/press-releases/half-of-global-wildlife-lost-says-new-wwf-report.

WWF projects more than a third of the world's population will face fresh water shortages by 2025.[19]

Even if overstated, these trends are massively disruptive—a virtual outgoing tide of economic potential. Coming at a time when the UN projects world population to grow from 6 billion people (1999) to 9.7 billion by 2050, they pose immense challenges to corporate managers and government economic planners.[20]

To reverse that outgoing tide and put the world economy back on a more regenerative course, a critical mass of companies will have to adopt Novo's life-mimicking attributes and culture. And they must do it quickly.

This won't be easy. As the Earth's resources get run down, raw material costs will rise. Global financial markets, already overburdened by high and rising debt/GDP ratios, will be strained. Company failure rates will accelerate. (Over the last 50 years, the average life-span of S&P 500 companies has shrunk from around 60 years to 18 years.)

Nevertheless, adaptive change is possible. Growth is not dead. Like Novo, we can and must think differently.

Most thinking employees today are generally aware of the resource and social challenges their companies must contend with. However, Novo goes a step further by ensuring that all employees are very well informed. Rather than hiding the truth from them, it addresses the difficult facts of planetary life head on.

Instead of becoming overwhelmed and depressed, Novo's employees respect this honesty and eagerly join in pursuing the company's

---

19   WWF (2016). Freshwater: what's at stake, what we're missing, what we're losing, what it's worth. Retrieved from http://wwf.panda.org/about_our_earth/about_freshwater/importance_value/.

20   United Nations (2015, July 29). World population projected to reach 9.7 billion by 2050. Retrieved from http://www.un.org/en/development/desa/news/population/2015-report.html.

transcendent goals. As they come to understand the imminent and pressing value of their work, employees become more committed, more adept at engaging their spiritual intelligence. This is where ethics, resource conservation, and shareholder growth unite. And judging from Novo's success, it is a prodigious union.

5

Openness

Henkel, a world leader in applied chemistry and adhesives technology, is unique in having its management board—consisting
of the CEO and five executive vice presidents—as "personally

---

1   Peter Senge (1990). *The Fifth Discipline: The Art and Practice of the Learn-
     ing Organization*. New York, NY: Currency Doubleday, p. 284.
2   Henkel (2008). *132 Years Quality from Henkel*, slide 6 Retrieved from http://
     www.slideshare.net/Henkel08/henkels-presentation.

liable partners."[3] With their own finances on the line, by company tradition, these six set a tone of personal commitment and open communication that permeates every part of the company.

Because commitment and openness are integral to learning and idea sharing, the continuity of such qualities over the years has endowed the company with an extraordinary breadth of vision, a world-class learning culture, elite sustainability ratings, and market-leading shareholder returns.

Today it manifests in a culture that openly engages the ideas and insights of all employees, making Henkel one of the world's most popular employers according to a variety of surveys, including the international Top Employers Institute.

Henkel's record between the turn of the millennium and year-end 2015 speaks volumes about the productivity and sustainability of its culture. During this period, while lowering the ecological footprint of its manufacturing operations and end-products, its common stock grew more than 450% in US$ terms—roughly nine times the S&P 500 Index—and its dividend increased fourfold. In common with other life-mimicking companies profiled in this book, it generated these results with little or no debt leverage. At year-end 2015, its balance sheet had more cash than debt.

Henkel is also widely acknowledged as a global ethics and sustainability leader. In January 2015, it featured for the sixth consecutive year in the Global Sustainability 100 and, for the eighth consecutive year, it was one of only 50 companies included in the elite Global Challenges Index. Henkel has been in the Dow Jones Sustainability Index every year since that index was founded in

---

3   Henkel is a *Kommanditgesellschaft auf Aktien* (KGaA). In terms of legal structure, a KGaA is a mixture of a joint stock corporation (AG) and a limited partnership (KG), with a focus in stock corporation law. Executive responsibility is vested in Henkel Management AG, the company's five-member management board, as the sole personally liable partner.

1999—eight times as a sector leader. Also in 2015, for the eighth consecutive time it was designated by Ethisphere.com as one of the "world's most ethical" companies.

There is a pattern to this story that becomes increasingly familiar as we look into the cultures of life-mimicking companies. It reveals that firms with open, ethical, inclusive traditions—where employees have a voice and a stake in what happens—have a distinct advantage over traditionally managed companies where most decisions are made at the top. In Henkel's case, by engaging the senses and intellects of 52,000 committed employees, it operates with a more broadly systemic view of its business ecosystem than a small cadre of top executives ever could.

Founded as a family enterprise in 1876, Henkel has survived and thrived for well over a century—through economic depressions, two world wars, disruptive technologies, and ecological challenges—because of this very openness and spirit of partnering. Today, when few companies survive more than 20 years, its story is compelling.

To the corporate historian Christian Stadler, long-lived companies have traditions of being "intelligently conservative," of approaching change in a "culturally sensitive manner ... that displays deep respect and understanding of existing mores and practices inside the organization."[4] In Henkel's case, those mores and practices are rooted in an organic sense of community and family that have guided the firm for generations. Today these are condensed into a brief Code of Teamwork and Leadership that describes its standards for open idea sharing and feedback: standards that empower employees to question assumptions and explore

---

4   Christian Stadler (2011, March 7). 5 ways to keep your company alive. *Fortune*. Retrieved from http://fortune.com/2011/03/07/5-ways-to-keep-your -company-alive/.

new solutions, and that expect leaders to value differences of opinion in an atmosphere of respectful listening and tolerance.

> Leaders establish a relationship of mutual trust, shaped by respect and tolerance. Conflicts are openly addressed in an objective and factual manner.
>
> Henkel, *Code of Teamwork and Leadership*[5]

Making people's lives better

Henkel's open inclusive traditions reflect the humanistic worldview (*Weltanschauung*) and vision of its founder, Fritz Henkel, which was to "make people's lives easier, better and more beautiful." More than a marketing theme, this has been the heart of a progressive management philosophy that Henkel and its founding family have maintained since 1876.

From the beginning, Fritz Henkel managed by the Golden Rule of reciprocity. As his company grew from a small family venture into a large corporation, he pushed the boundaries of *laissez-faire* capitalism, which in too many instances allowed business owners to freely exploit employees.

To make the lives of employees better, Henkel was one of the first companies to:

- Offer in-plant health clinics (1912)

- Establish an elected employee representative council (1917)

---

5   Henkel (2009). *Vision and Values: Code of Teamwork and Leadership*, p. 5. Retrieved from http://www.henkel-adhesives.com/com/content_data/188315_Code_of_Teamwork_and_Leadership.pdf.

- Create a pension fund for "old age and surviving dependents" (1918)

- Invite salaried workers onto its Supervisory Board (1924)

- Initiate employee bonuses for suggestions leading to improvements in occupational safety (1929)

Although during World War II, like all German companies, Henkel had to comply with the wishes of the German government—by using prisoners and forced labor in its factories to replace employees sent to the front—when the war ended, it returned to its progressive ways.

During the postwar era of reconstruction, Henkel broadened its theme of making people's lives better by becoming an environmental leader. Ahead of its competitors, it introduced a system of ecological quality checks for detergents and household cleaners (1959). Later, as its environmental expertise grew, it became one of the first companies to initiate a system of internal ecological audits (1988) and to develop a dedicated research subsidiary for developing safe biotechnologies (Cognis, 1991).

In 1992, prior to the Rio Earth Summit, Henkel issued its first environmental report. Rather than adopting a public relations stance, it offered detailed technical accounts of its production processes and the safety of its products, thereby opening itself to feedback and criticism from diverse stakeholders, including the scientific community. Although such openness carried potential liability risks, Henkel's personally liable executive partners thought the benefits to its learning capacity outweighed those risks.

As the global environmental movement evolved into a more comprehensive sustainability movement, Henkel broadened its concept of making people's lives better. In 2003, it became one of the first multinationals to sign the UN Global Compact on human rights, fair labor practices, environmental responsibility, and anticorruption. From that year onward those standards were incorporated into all of its annual reports.

As Henkel's annual reporting evolved, the company began to show the connections between its sustainability practices, risk mitigation, and profitability. Called "integrated reporting," this enabled stakeholders to see in a more granular way how sustainability contributes to customer and shareholder value.

To emphasize these connections and make them central to Henkel's corporate strategy, Kasper Rorsted, who became CEO in April 2008, developed a goal called "Factor-3" that set a 20-year goal of "tripling the value we create through our business activities in relation to our environmental footprint."[6] Introduced in 2010—a time when the world was emerging from a deep recession caused in large part by unsustainable ecological and economic business practices—it was a moral call to action, a message to all stakeholders that making people's lives easier, better, and more beautiful was more than a company slogan. It was Henkel's reason for being.

Factor-3 goals

In explaining the new Factor-3 goals, management made it clear there were two ways to do this. One is to "triple the value we create while leaving the footprint at the same level," while the other is to "reduce our ecological footprint to one third of today's level."[7] The ideal was to approach Factor-3 from both sides, reducing raw material input and improving output at the same time with the net result

6   Henkel (2014). Our ambitious targets for 2030. Retrieved from http://sustainabilityreport2013.henkel.com/strategy/goal-for-2030-factor-3/.
7   Ibid.

being to use one third of the resources needed today for each Euro of revenue generated.

In so stating its options, Henkel emphasized the inspiring management by means (MBM) goal of reducing its adverse impacts rather than the more stressful management by results (MBR) goal of having to grow sales at an accelerated pace. This message was further affirmed by giving more weight to employee safety, health, and environment (SHE) goals than to growing sales.

To help employees imagine achieving the Factor-3 goal in 20 years, Henkel created five-year targets. The first, encompassing the years 2011 to 2015, was to "improve the relationship between the value we create and our ecological footprint by 30 percent overall"[8]— a goal that anticipated efficiency gains averaging 5–6% each year. Inspired by this goal, which gave employees a transcendent sense of purpose, Henkel work teams eagerly took up the challenge. By year-end 2015, they had exceeded the initial five-year target by achieving improvements of 38%.

To underscore the seriousness of the world's growing ecological deficit, Henkel also committed to "Factor-5" efficiencies by 2050. Strategically, it was a way to emphasize the extreme urgency of this goal as a long-term proposition. It said, in effect, that if Henkel and the planet were to have a sustainable future—especially as the world population placed additional strains on the Earth's resources and climate—environmental goals would have to be front and center.

Based on results achieved so far, Rorsted's strategy has been financially successful as well as meeting Henkel's SHE goals. From the inception of Factor-3 in 2010 to the end of its first five-year phase, the company increased its returns on capital employed from 14.9% in 2010 to 18.2% on the strength of market share and operating efficiency gains. During this time Henkel's shares grew in

8   Ibid.

value by 120%—nearly double the MSCI and FTSE world indices and more than triple the shares of Procter & Gamble, its nearest corporate comparator.

> The global human footprint is already greater today than the planet's resources can bear. ... [W]e are already using up resources faster than our planet can replenish them. And this situation will get dramatically worse in the coming decades. Sacrificing consumption or quality of life is not a realistic solution. What we have to do is find ways to achieve more with less. And that is exactly what our new strategy is all about.
>
> Kasper Rorsted, CEO, Henkel[9]

Safety, health, and environment goals

Henkel's ability to surpass the Factor-3 objectives of its first five-year plan was largely due to substantial progress made on its SHE goals. In spite of increasing the volume of company sales by 9%, it made absolute reductions in its ecological footprint and substantially increased the safety of employees along its value chain. According to independently audited results published in its 2015 sustainability report, the following results were achieved:

- Energy consumption down 20%

- CO_2 emissions down 19%

9   Kasper Rorsted (2010). Sustainability strategy: interview with Kasper Rorsted, CEO. Retrieved from http://www.loctite.at/atd/content_data/373296_interviewsustainabilitystrategykasperrorsted.pdf.

- Volatile organic compound emissions down 22%
- Water consumption down 19%
- Volume of waste-water down 30%
- Chemical oxygen demand to waste-water down 36%
- Heavy metals emissions to waste-water down 37%
- Waste for recycling and disposal down 18%
- Occupational accidents among Henkel employees down 25%
- Occupational accidents among supplier employees down 20%

To achieve its environmental goals, all Henkel products are subject to life-cycle analyses that estimate their ecological footprint, from the selection of raw materials through manufacturing, packaging, transport, and all activities involved with retailing and shopping, as well as use by consumers and final disposal.

In selecting raw materials, Henkel seeks those that are ecologically benign and renewable. It also uses its influence as a major world buyer of agricultural commodities to protect the Earth's climate and biological resources. A good example of this proactive approach is the way it purchases palm oil—an inexpensive biodegradable surfactant used in laundry detergents and cosmetics.

Seeing how the world's growing demand for palm oil had become an ecological disaster as opportunistic producers slashed and burned large tracts of tropical rainforest to make room for monoculture plantations—practices that accelerated climate change, destroyed thousands of species, and disrupted the lives of millions who depended on the forest for their livelihoods—Henkel decided to take affirmative action.

Consequently in 2003, it joined Unilever and became a charter member of the Roundtable on Sustainable Palm Oil (RSPO) with a pledge to procure in phased steps its entire supplies of this raw material from ecologically responsible suppliers. In 2008, it became the first company to cover selected products with tradable RSPO certificates that ensure their supplies do not contribute to net deforestation. By year-end 2015 all Henkel products were covered by those certificates. To reinforce its quest to fight global deforestation and protect biodiversity, it has also signed a Consumer Goods Forum pledge to achieve a goal of "zero net deforestation" by 2020.

> Since we purchase our surfactants from raw material suppliers, we are at the end of a long supply chain. By buying certificates, we can provide support for sustainable palm oil production in the growing countries. This is because the certificates give plantation operators an economic incentive to produce palm oil sustainably.
> Henkel, Report to RSPO, 2013/14[10]

In conformity with its life-affirming ecological goals, Henkel is also committed to the safety of employees and those who work for suppliers. To achieve targeted occupational safety results under its SHE goals, it requires all company facilities to continuously monitor accidents and health conditions; many offer counseling on stress and conflict management as well. In support of best practices, company physicians and human resource officials meet annually to

10   Henkel (2014). *Annual Communication of Progress 2013/2014*. Retrieved from http://www.rspo.org/file/acop2014/submissions/henkel-ag-co-kgaa-ACOP2014.pdf.

discuss results and ideas for improvement, with findings made available to all sites worldwide.

One area of particular concern is protecting the skin of employees, customers, and all who come into contact with Henkel products. Questions regarding the effects of Henkel products on skin are investigated by *in vitro* tests (alternatives to animal testing), the results of which are submitted to the European Union Reference Laboratory for Alternatives to Animal Testing and openly shared with other biologists and lab technicians as a matter of transcendent principle.

To further expand its knowledge of sustainability practices, Henkel and five other European chemical companies established in 2011 an initiative called "Together for Sustainability—The Chemical Initiative for Sustainable Supply Chains" (TfS). The aim of the initiative was to harmonize increasingly complex supply chain management processes and to optimize dialogue among worldwide business partners, supported by uniform web-based performance reports. Based on established principles of the UN Global Compact, the Responsible Care Global Charter, the International Labour Organization, and Social Accountability International, TfS standards are backed by independent expert audits. In recognition of its cost-effectiveness and success in promoting supply chain best practices, the number of TfS members tripled in 2015 from the original six to 18.

The big picture we get from Henkel's implementation of Factor-3 is a company that has set new standards for corporate ethics and productivity across a broad spectrum. This has had a compounding effect both within the firm—via the reinforcing cycle of LAS—and externally as the influences of its ideas and practices have spread.

This dynamic has made Henkel a globally preferred employer and one of the 50 most popular in Europe—an intangible asset that ensures a continuous flow of qualified talent.

Accountability

Given the sense of urgency Kasper Rorsted felt about lowering Henkel's ecological footprint and spreading sustainability best practices, he and his management team introduced in 2009 a set of policies to decentralize and accelerate decision-making by making managers more accountable—in effect treating them more like partners than well-paid staff. If the company was to meet its goals, everyone had to be engaged, to feel a sense of personal responsibility.

In common with all deeply life-mimicking companies, this decentralization strategy enabled Henkel to be small (locally autonomous) and big at the same time. By spreading responsibility across many decision points, employees began to feel more valued, more engaged, and more responsible for their professional development. Further, by framing Factor-3 as an ethical mission—a practical way out of the ecological trap that industrial capitalism had set for itself—Rorsted gave them a transcendent sense of purpose that their lives and ideas mattered greatly.

In concept and execution, this new accountability standard became a social compact focused on the health of the whole. As noted in a classic 2012 Harvard Business School case study,[11] all Henkel managers were to be evaluated annually based on their leadership skills, professional development, and value-added contributions.

Evaluations were made by development roundtables (DRTs), where senior managers would assess the performance and leadership potential of leaders who served on their teams and score them on their contributions to company goals. While, on the surface, this approach seems mechanistic and rigid, in execution it has been

---

11   Robert Simons & Natalie Kindred (2012). Henkel: Building a Winning Culture. Harvard Business School case 9-112-060, rev. April 14, 2012.

holistic, flexible, and democratic. By letting people know face-to-face how they are performing in terms of effort, commitment, and results, it gives them a chance to learn and improve. And most do.

From a corporate development perspective, the DRTs have made it easier for senior executives to identify top performers and find ways to mentor them. The roundtables also encourage managers at lower levels to give top performers stretch assignments and growth opportunities.

Under a companion system of key performance indicators (KPIs), each year the top management sets two or three goals at the company level (operating margin, organic sales growth, innovation, customer focus, etc.), which become standards for evaluating performance at the group and team levels. KPI scores range from zero (no progress) through 100% (targets achieved) up to 200% (meaning targets are substantially passed). Individual performance then becomes an amalgam of the DRT score and individual KPIs, and bonuses are made accordingly.

Because managerial employees were engaged in developing this evaluation system, it became a tacit compact—a matter of faith concerning the future welfare of the company and attainment of its sustainability goals. By this standard, those who did not believe in the compact—many of whom were managers accustomed to a more relaxed style of management—had to be let go in favor of employees who welcomed, and thrived in, the new environment.

Everyone who didn't want to play under the new rules was asked to leave. Around 50% of our top 180 executives, including the management board, have changed in the past three years; the majority of the new people, more than 75%, were appointed from within. A lot of young people got promoted to take on new responsibility—and this has injected new vitality into the organization.

Kasper Rorsted, CEO, Henkel[12]

Rather than being heartless, the compact looked to the greater good of sustainability and returning business to a more life-affirming path. According to the renowned management authority, Charles Handy, such actions are fundamentally democratic. "If someone can no longer be trusted" to uphold agreed common rules, "he or she cannot be given an empty space."[13] Otherwise, the compact becomes meaningless.

To Rorsted's credit, the new accountability rules kept the primary focus on capacity building (means) rather than financial performance (results). By helping managerial staff grow via constructive feedback and mentoring, and by inspiring them with a transcendent vision of the future, he got Factor-3 off to a fast start in terms of both sustainability and financial performance.

The value of clarity and transparency

Henkel's capacity to meet and surpass its first five-year Factor-3 goal owes much to its culture of clarity and transparency. Managers know where they and their teams stand in relation to specific goals via the openly democratic processes of DRT and KPI assessments.

12   Quoted in Robert Simons & Natalie Kindred (2012). Henkel: Building a Winning Culture. Harvard Business School case 9-112-060, rev. April 14, 2012, p. 12.

13   Charles Handy (1998). *Beyond Certainty: The Changing Worlds of Organizations*. Boston, MA: Harvard Business School Press, pp. 52-53.

The company's intranet and website provide current, often up-to-the-minute, information on Factor-3 and SHE performance for the benefit of all stakeholders. External audits of company and sub-contractor facilities are made public as a means of verifying compliance with ethical standards and identifying risks that need to be addressed.

Attesting to the openness of Henkel's annual reports, the League of American Communications Professionals has consistently rated them in the world's "top 100" for quality and content. For 2014, Henkel's annual financial and sustainability reports won awards with scores of 99 and 96 respectively out of 100. Beyond securing shareholder loyalty, these reports also generate trust among business partners and within the communities where the company operates.

With so much critical information out in the open, little time is wasted on ambiguities and misunderstandings, enabling decisions to be made at a faster pace. Such was the case when Henkel negotiated its 2004 acquisition of Dial (a U.S. company with compatible personal care and household product lines). In describing the talks leading to the final agreement, Herbert Baum, Dial's CEO at the time, relates a conversation he had with Albrecht Woeste, Henkel's nonexecutive chairman and great-grandson of company founder Fritz Henkel, prior to the deal: "We didn't talk about money and we didn't talk about the agreement, we talked about corporate culture, and [ensuring] the people at Dial keep their jobs."[14]

To Baum, these assurances were credible because Henkel's ethics and care for employees were an open book. This engendered a spirit of trust that enabled the companies to merge operations with a

14   Quoted in Herbert Baum & Tammy Kling (2009). *The Transparent Leader: How to Build a Great Company Through Straight Talk, Openness and Accountability*. New York, NY: HarperCollins ebooks, p. 128.

minimum of friction. In hindsight, the $2.9 billion deal was a multiple win: good for both companies, their employees, customers, and shareholders alike.

Self-reinvention

The story of Henkel's entry into the adhesives business—currently its largest and most profitable product line—offers deeper insight into its culture of openness and entrepreneurship, which has enabled it to adapt and reinvent itself with remarkable speed. It begins in 1923, during founder Fritz Henkel's lifetime, when a supplier of glue for product labels was forced to interrupt deliveries. Rather than looking for an alternative supplier, company employees used their knowledge of applied chemistry and their manufacturing know-how to quickly fill the gap.

Although originally intended as an in-house service, Henkel's chemists quickly saw new revenue opportunities. From the time they started researching starch-based adhesives in March until Henkel started manufacturing them in June, barely four months passed. By year-end 1923, just six months later, it had produced 170 tons, much of which was sold to a neighboring company. (This likely influenced Henkel's decision to invite employees onto the company's Supervisory Board in 1924.) Over the next five years, after building out and improving the product line, adhesives became a competitive source of export revenues.

Although interrupted by the Great Depression and World War II, Henkel quickly revived its adhesives business in 1946 to meet the growing demands of postwar reconstruction and industrial development. As its sales grew in the 1950s, the Henkel family's tradition of social responsibility became more evident in its product offers.

This led to the ecological quality checks for detergents and household cleaners (1959) already noted, and later to the introduction of Pritt (1969), a solvent-free glue which is now a global bestseller.

As Henkel's reputation for ethics, quality, and eco-innovation grew, other companies took notice. One such was Loctite, whose products (anaerobic sealants) also conveyed ecological benefits by saving time, energy, and waste in manufacturing and repair operations. To thwart a hostile takeover by Allied Signal in the mid-1980s, Loctite offered Henkel a 35% stake in the company. Seeing the potential synergies between the two firms, Henkel quickly agreed.

A decade later, in November 1996, Henkel offered to buy the remaining 65%. Once again, the decision to proceed came quickly. Moved by its open, progressive, and innovative culture, Loctite's leadership agreed and the deal was consummated two months later.

In April 2008, Henkel completed another major acquisition within only three months, buying from Akzo Nobel its National Starch Adhesives and Electronic Materials businesses for €3.7 billion ($5.6 billion) in cash. Abetted by Henkel's reputation for openness and transparency, the deal was again quickly consummated on fair terms for both parties.

The common threads in these stories of entrepreneurship and self-reinvention are deeply rooted in Henkel's history of making peoples lives "easier, better and more beautiful," and by being prepared to move quickly on opportunities to fulfill its mission.

Today roughly 30% of sales from Henkel's Adhesives Technology group come from products less than five years old. One of the most promising of these is an eco-friendly line of bio-adhesives (mainly plant-based), where Henkel is again the global innovation leader.

With a fast and transparent decision process, we
clearly define accountability and responsibility, so
that we avoid fatigue and stimulate motivation.
Hans Von Bylen, Executive
Vice President, Henkel[15]

Enduring qualities

Like all companies profiled in this book, Henkel has long understood that its capacity to innovate relies on its speed of learning,
which in turn relies on the openness and inclusiveness of its culture.

Inclusion, an attribute of openness, recognizes that the diversity
of ideas (species) endows systems (both natural and corporate)
with strength that eludes monocultures. Today Henkel draws its
employees from over 120 nations with 57% coming from emerging
markets, where it has been expanding its presence. Women comprise 33% of management positions and are broadly represented on
Henkel's Supervisory Board (including Board Chair, Dr. Simone
Bagel-Trah).

Vice President Kathrin Menges, one of Henkel's six personally
liable executive leaders, calls diversity a "strategic asset" because
"finding and implementing ... better—even revolutionary—solutions ... is possible only when the widest spectrum of mindsets,
attitudes, beliefs, abilities and personalities work together."[16]

---

15   Quoted in Robert Simons & Natalie Kindred (2012). Henkel: Building a Winning Culture. Harvard Business School case 9-112-060, rev. April 14, 2012,
p. 14.
16   Henkel (n.d.) One Henkel: Global Diversity & Inclusion, p. 9. Retrieved
from http://docplayer.net/docview/24/3370172/#file=/storage/24/3370172/
3370172.pdf.

For employees, being exposed to diverse ideas on work teams enables them to think more critically: to reflect beyond *what* they observe to *why*. Called double-loop learning, this capacity to continually "reflect while doing" greatly speeds the rate at which Henkel adapts to changing market conditions. As a result, employees are quicker to spot errors and inconvenient truths before these become ossified within the system.

Such openness is increasingly important today in adapting to the complexities of global markets, where information flows quickly via social media and where there is a continuous threat of disruptive events. Compared with the mid-19th century when Henkel was founded, the world is vastly more crowded and urbanized, more ecologically stressed, more exposed to technology change, more financially leveraged, more politically unstable, and generally more chaotic. Such complexities make it more important than ever to see systems as a whole by having thoughtful, intelligent people on the ground where change is happening and to vest those people with the authority to make decisions quickly as conditions change.

To maintain such levels of awareness, Henkel launched in 2012 an innovative "Sustainability Ambassadors" program. The idea behind it was to imbue employees with a clear understanding of sustainability and enable them to convey its importance to others. Focused on educating school children—the next generation of consumers—it compels employees to think clearly and simply, and be more aware of Henkel's impacts in local markets. As a systems thinking initiative, the program was insightful because the act of teaching automatically engages the teacher in listening, observing, and learning through local dialogue—the very qualities needed to transcend workplace issues, and to see and think more holistically.

> [Our program] has trained around 6,200 Sustainability Ambassadors—including all Management Board members—in 74 countries. Ambassadors are encouraged to visit elementary schools in order to explain the concept of sustainability by means of simple, everyday examples. Since the start of the program, the Sustainability Ambassadors have helped to educate around 63,000 schoolchildren in 43 countries.
>
> Henkel, *Annual Report*, 2015[17]

Returning to the historian Christian Stadler's observations about long-lived companies, Henkel has been fortunate in having a founding family that maintains a tradition of being "intelligently conservative," and of approaching change in a "culturally sensitive manner." Because of this galvanizing ethic, the company has been continually open to feedback from employees, customers, suppliers, and host communities—an attentive quality that has enabled it to learn and adapt faster than most of its global corporate peers.

Influence of the Henkel family

Although family members no longer manage Henkel, they retain 53.65% of the company's voting stock, which gives them effective control. While some people regard such concentrated control as insular and limiting, the company is, in fact, one of the world's most open to stakeholder feedback and adaptive innovation.

---

17 Henkel (2016). *Annual Report 2015*, p. 27. Retrieved from http://www. henkel.com/investors-and-analysts/financial-reports/annual-reports.

Starting with Fritz Henkel's invitations to employees to serve on representative councils (1917) and on Henkel's Supervisory Board (1924) through to its diverse, inclusive culture today, it retains a unique flexibility and capacity to learn.

Further, with voting control in secure hands, Henkel has fewer distractions from corporate raiders who seek short-term profits at the expense of long-term stakeholders: the employees, customers, suppliers, and host communities for whom it seeks to make life "better, easier and more beautiful." Consequently, like Novo Nordisk—where voting control resides with the Novo Foundation—Henkel is freer to chart it own course.

Henkel's two-board structure also serves to maintain its open culture. Its 16-member Supervisory Board—made up of an equal number of shareholder and employee representatives—regularly advises and monitors its Management Board of six "personally liable partners" in their stewardship of the company. Headed by Dr. Simone Bagel-Trah, a Henkel family member, it represents a diversity of experience and perspective that keeps the firm in alignment with its traditional roots of stakeholder service.

In partnership with the Shareholders' Committee, which represents the interests of nonfamily shareholders, these boards serve a checks-and-balances function guided by three principles:

1. Value creation as the foundation of the company's management approach

2. Sustainability achieved through the application of socially responsible management principles

3. Transparency supported by an active and open information policy

The interactions between these three bodies are described on Henkel's corporate website as follows:

The Management Board agrees on the strategic direction
of the company with the Shareholders' Committee and dis-
cusses with it the status of strategy implementation at regular
intervals. In keeping with good corporate management practice, the Management Board informs the Supervisory Board
and the Shareholders' Committee regularly, and in a timely
and comprehensive fashion, of all relevant issues concerning
business policy, corporate planning, profitability, the business development of the corporation and its major affiliated
companies, and also matters relating to risk exposure and risk
management.[18]

On paper this hybrid structure sounds complex. But, like large,
complex ecosystems in Nature, it functions well because it is open
at multiple levels to feedback from within the system and unified by
values that serve the health of the system as a whole. By such means,
as Henkel approaches its 140th birthday, it keeps getting better with
age.

18 Henkel (2016). Management and corporate boards. Retrieved from http://
www.henkel.com/company/management-corporate-boards.

6

Sense of purpose

Profit is not the explanation, cause or rationale of business behavior and business decisions, but rather the test of their validity.

Peter Drucker[1]

It took us a while, but we finally figured out that we could ... bring about environmental, labor and social change ... We saw that doing the right thing was good for business today—and would be an engine for our growth in the near future. With each new discovery and partnership, we willingly gave up old ideas to shift our thinking toward a

---

1   Peter F. Drucker (2001). *The Essential Drucker: The Best of Sixty Years of Peter Drucker's Essential Writings on Management*. New York, NY: HarperCollins, p. 18. Reproduced by kind permission of HarperCollins and the Peter F. Drucker Literary Trust.

better, smarter, faster and ultimately more sustainable future—financially, environmentally and
socially.

Mark Parker, President and CEO, Nike[2]

In 2004, Nike formally integrated corporate responsibility into its
business strategy. Already a global leader in progressive labor practices, closed-loop manufacturing, supply chain management, community economic development, and charitable giving, the company
decided to shift its emphasis from "risk management, philanthropy
and compliance to one that utilizes our natural focus on innovation to ... [bring] people, planet and profits into balance for lasting
success."[3]

To CEO Mark Parker, sustainability is a strategic priority, central
to Nike's capacity to grow profitably. The firm's strategy, as stated
above, is essentially based on the reinforcing cycle of living asset
stewardship (LAS), where inspiring goals catalyze learning, innovation, and profit.

Understanding the systemic nature of "doing the right thing," as
Parker framed it, Nike has evolved into a radically decentralized
and networked culture of open information sharing. Employees at
all levels are empowered to make quick decisions. The primary role
of team leaders is to "coach and inspire" by "[h]oning the ability of

2   Mark Parker (2009). Letter from the CEO. In Nike, *Corporate Responsibility
    Report 2007–2009* (pp. 4-5), p. 4. Retrieved from http://www.fibre2fashion.
    com/sustainability/pdf/nikesustainabilityreport.pdf.

3   Nike (2009). *Corporate Responsibility Report 2007–2009*, p. 22. Retrieved
    from http://www.fibre2fashion.com/sustainability/pdf/nikesustainability
    report.pdf.

employees to ask the right questions, examining learning opportunities, and continually rethinking the needs of the business."[4]

Reflecting management faith in open employee engagement, in
2005 Nike conducted a company-wide dialogue on sustainability,
challenging employees through group exercises and brainstorming
sessions to define how the future could look, how Nike would get
there, and employees' roles in creating that future.

The same open interactive networking process also extends to
external stakeholders. Realizing that the challenges of today's
increasingly resource-constrained world are beyond the capacity of
any single company to solve, Nike collaborates with other companies (including competitors), plus governments, universities, and
NGOs, and, as we shall see, contributes much of its technical expertise to open-source platforms.

Like all LAMP companies, there is a symbiotic pattern to this
internal and external quest for partnership: a sense of mutuality
that we're all in this together, that solutions will only come if we
pool our intellectual resources and consider the systemic nature of
our resource challenges.

The success of this broadly systemic approach, as seen throughout this book, is clear. Companies that deeply mimic life have
become market share and profit leaders because they live and work
in closer harmony with the larger living systems in which we exist
(society, biosphere); and the deeper they go in this direction the
more inspiring, innovative, and successful they become.

Nike's leadership in this corporate movement is reflected in its
regular inclusion in *CR Magazine*'s annual "100 Best Corporate

---

4   Nike (2011). *FY10/11 Sustainable Business Performance Summary*, p. 72.
    Retrieved from https://www.unglobalcompact.org/system/attachments/
    15435/original/NIKE_SUSTAINABLE_BUSINESS_REPORT_FY10-11_
    FINAL.pdf?.

Citizens" (#38 in 2015), and the Dow Jones Sustainability and FTSE4Good indices. The quality and transparency of its sustainability reporting have also earned top honors from the Corporate Register Reporting Awards ("First Runner Up," 2015).

With such leadership attributes, Nike naturally attracts and retains talented people—employees with a desire to make a difference through learning and action. Since 2009, when Glassdoor commenced its "Best Places to Work" list, Nike has been in the "top 50" five times (#25 in 2015). In recognition of the creativity generated by this talent pool, *Fast Company* magazine has six times rated Nike among the world's "top 50" innovative companies since 2007 (#1 in 2013, #17 in 2014).

On the strength of these qualities, Nike has become a global profit leader. From the turn of the century through year-end 2015, its share price and dividend grew roughly tenfold—more than 20 times the S&P 500, which grew by less than 50%. With more than $4.67 billion of net cash on its balance sheet at year-end 2015 and net operating cash flow of $4.68 billion, it has the resources and standing to remain a world-class learning center for sustainability innovation.

Learning from mistakes

One of the prime attributes of life-mimicking companies is their capacity to learn and grow from mistakes. Such was the case when Nike, stung by legitimate criticisms of labor and environmental problems at its contract plants in Asia and Central America, undertook reforms that set new standards for corporate responsibility and imbued the company with a new sense of purpose, where "workers across the industry are consistently valued, and environmental impact is a critical metric of success."[5]

The story of Nike's awakening begins in the early 1990s. At the time the company thought of itself as a "designer and marketer" of athletic wear—not a manufacturer—and so took a hands-off approach toward its contract plants in emerging Asia. However, when it came to light through a variety of media that these contractors used child labor, abused human rights, forced overtime in unhealthy, unsafe sweatshops, and violated local minimum wage and environmental rules—conditions that were antithetical to Nike's image of health and fitness—the criticism hit the company at the core of its value proposition.

After a first step to create a contractor code of conduct (1992) failed because of poor oversight and administration, Nike got serious. In 1993 it created an Environmental Action Team and several new departments, including one on Labor Practices—all of which were later organized under a Corporate Responsibility and Compliance Department (1998).

Working together for more than six years, these teams lay the groundwork toward what would become the Shambhala Action Learning Initiative (2000). From these internal dialogues—which reflect the emerging progressive ideals of its culture—Nike launched diverse company-wide change projects, which had transformative effects on its value chain management, its Design for Environment principles, its 2020 goals on closed-loop manufacturing, and ultimately its Product Sustainability Mission.

Looking back on this initiative a decade later, Darcy Winslow, one of the Shambahala team leaders, said: "The result of this one

5   Nike (2012, May 3). Nike's vision for a sustainable economy. Retrieved from http://extassets.nike.com/sponge_archives/2012/05/nikes_vision_for_a_ sustainable.php

year intensive helped transform Nike's approach to sustainability and created 100 internal champions who launched dozens of landmark projects that continue to deliver against our 2020 goals."[6]

As these change initiatives progressed, Nike joined the Global Alliance for Workers and Communities (1999) with a minimum five-year commitment and a \$7.8 million investment to better understand what workers think of their jobs and their lives. Such collaboration led to Nike fully disclosing the location of all its contract plants (2005), a program of regular audits, and a grading system for suppliers based on labor, environment, and health standards, which became the foundation of an incentive program that awarded best practice suppliers with more orders.

In 2000, Nike took further large steps toward ethical leadership by becoming one of the first multinational corporations to join the UN Global Compact and the World Wildlife Fund's (WWF) Climate Savers program: framework agreements that bound it to core standards on human rights, labor standards, environmental sustainability, and greenhouse gas emissions through all its operations, including contract manufacturers. To focus employees' attention on these goals, it also launched a company-wide training program centered on product sustainability, and initiated a program of sustainability metrics. Commenting on these new initiatives, CEO Phil Knight wrote in that year's annual report, "If we are to succeed, one universal truth is clear: We need to go through a re-commitment process."[7]

6   Greenopolis (2010, March 4). Team Shambhala: Nike's journey from wasted reputation to corporate responsibility. Retrieved from http://3blmedia. com/theCSRfeed/Team-Shambhala-Nike's-Journey-Wasted-Reputation-Corporate-Responsibility.

7   Phil Knight (2000). Letter to shareholders. Retrieved from http://media. corporate-ir.net/media_files/irol/10/100529/Areports/ar_00/letter.html.

The core of that recommitment was to move beyond compliance toward a values-based system that would become a source of inspiration throughout the firm. Writing in Nike's first Corporate Responsibility Report (October 2001), Maria Eitel, then Vice President and Senior Advisor for Corporate Responsibility said, "We've made a commitment to enter a new era of commerce where human and business needs don't deplete living systems."[8]

Today Nike has a three-tiered system of monitoring contract manufacturers' social responsibility, including:

- Employee teams dedicated to labor and environmental compliance who visit contract plants in all countries where its products are manufactured on a regular (sometimes daily) basis

- Embedded production specialists who are trained in Nike's code of conduct, labor practices, safety, health, and environment programs

- External audit firms including accredited non-profits (Verite and the Fair Labor Association)

Stepping back and looking at Nike's transformation since the early 1990s, the company clearly took to heart the criticisms it received about conditions in contract plants and used these to accomplish a paradigmatic shift in corporate consciousness: making respect for life a core ideal in all parts of its business instead of a peripheral matter for which contractors were not responsible. Like Nucor's transformation in the 1960s, where employees became the central focus of management attention, rather than a secondary concern, this paradigmatic shift infused Nike with new energy and

---

8   PRNewswire (2001, October 9). Nike releases first corporate responsibility report. Retrieved from http://www.prnewswire.com/news-releases/nike-releases-first-corporate-responsibility-report-73575257.html.

vaulted it into a position of innovation and productivity leadership. In both cases, the management showed qualities of empathy and deep caring that touched employees, inspiring them to learn and work with their hearts as well as their minds.

In doing so, Nike departed from traditional business practices by placing a higher value on living assets (people and Nature) than on nonliving capital assets. Even though it doesn't describe its transformation as such, respect for life became a coherent core ideal and an evolving growth path as the company became more adept at LAS.

As part of that evolution, Nike has become more symbiotic, realizing that it is part of a larger web of life on which it totally depends and creating a corporate sense of purpose around that realization. This required a deep dive into nonlinear systems thinking—understanding how intimately business, biosphere, and society are connected—and letting go of the linear bottom-line-first thinking that had come to define the Industrial Revolution.

Realizing that effecting meaningful change in such a complex interconnected global system is beyond the capacity of any one company acting on its own, Nike has become since 2008 a corporate leader in open-source collaboration, with a goal of bringing all business into closer harmony with Nature and society (a topic we will take up later).

Nike is a large company by most standards, but our ability to influence meaningful change at the systemic level has limitations. It is absolutely crucial that we work with other players to prompt real, sustainable system change. We embrace partnerships and open-source collaboration. We have proactively shared our sustainable design

> tools to help create an industry standard and
> continue to look for ways to scale innovations at
> Nike and across our industry.
>
> Mark Parker, President and CEO, Nike[9]

Symbiosis as strategic catalyst

Symbiosis is a quality inherent in all life and living systems. At a minimum, it describes relationships where individuals derive benefit from one another. This is called "mutualism." In companies that mimic life, as in Nature, it also encompasses processes that serve the health of the total living system in which they exist. For companies, that larger system includes the biosphere and society.

Examples of such symbiotic practices at Nike include a number of cross-sector collaborations that address major systemic problems, such as climate change, ecological overstep, and poverty:

- BICEP (Business for Innovative Climate & Energy Policy) created in 2008, in collaboration with the Coalition for Environmentally Responsible Economies (CERES): a coalition of 20 consumer brand companies committed to advancing meaningful energy and climate legislation that will enable a rapid transition to a low-carbon, 21st-century economy, thereby creating new jobs and stimulating economic growth while stabilizing the Earth's fragile climate

- GAMECHANGERS, a revolving fund created in 2009 with Architecture for Humanity to build sustainable and

---

9   Nike (2012). *Corporate Responsibility Report 2012*, p. 4. Retrieved from https://www.scribd.com/document/95032587/Nike-Sustainable-Business -Report-Fy10-11-Final.

safe places to play for children in communities that lack resources, with an emphasis on at-risk youth and using sports as a catalyst for social and economic empowerment

- The GreenXchange, created in 2010 with the non-profit Creative Commons, through which companies share ideas and technologies with varying degrees of intellectual property protection, thereby catalyzing improvements on a greater scale than any company could achieve by acting alone

- The Sustainable Apparel Coalition, a consortium created in 2011 comprising 85 companies (including some competitors) and 17 organizations representing NGOs, governments, and universities dedicated to creating a common approach for measuring and evaluating sustainability performance

- The Plant (PET) Technology Working Group, created in 2012 in collaboration with Coca-Cola, Ford, Heinz, and Procter & Gamble to accelerate the development and use of 100% plant-based PET materials and fiber in their products

- The LAUNCH 2020 Summit—convened in 2013 in collaboration with NASA, the U.S. Agency for International Development, the U.S. Department of State, materials specialists, designers, academics, manufacturers, entrepreneurs, and NGOs—to catalyze action around the sustainability of materials with a goal of transforming processes for producing fabrics

In each of these collaborations, Nike contributes both valuable intellectual resources and financial support. In support of the Sustainable Apparel Coalition, for example, it has shared its expertise in environmental design and sustainable materials to create an open-source information-sharing platform called the Higg Index. Formed in 2012, this index enables companies to assess their products through an entire life-cycle with a scoring system based on best practices, plus a rating system for material vendors. Modified in 2013, the Higg Index also includes social/labor best practice tools.

Because of Nike's contributions to the Higg Index, Deloitte in 2012 named it one of six exemplary global "ecosystem players."[10] Selection criteria included "holistic strategic vision," supported by "measurable and ambitious mid- to long-term targets" toward creating "shared value by … involving their suppliers and other stakeholders in their actions."

In addition to these symbiotic practices focused on mutual benefit, Nike also employs a commensal form of symbiosis, in which it uses free biospheric resources—wind and solar energy—without creating either mutual benefit or harm (parasitism) to those resources. As a corporate goal, this too fits the ecological metaphor. Although one can argue that the resources consumed in building solar and wind energy systems deplete environmental resources, over their productive lifetimes these renewable energy systems are robustly net positive.

The important point to remember about both symbiotic practices at Nike is their leaning toward the positive aspects of symbiosis (mutualism, commensalism) and away from the negative (parasitic) ones that have long been the industrial norm.

The operating leverage in such practices, as we have seen throughout this book, resides in the human psyche. As employees connect their work to their higher ideals and biophilic instincts, they engage their spiritual intelligence, which guides their IQ and emotional

10   Deloitte (2012). *Towards Zero Impact Growth: Strategies of Leading Companies in 10 Industries*, pp. 15-16. Retrieved from https://www.mkb.nl/sites/default/files/downloadables_vno/deloitte_csr_onderzoek_0.pdf.

intelligence by giving each a sense of meaning and direction. The effectiveness of this higher intelligence is affirmed by Nike's exemplary environmental, social, and financial performance.

The motive behind Nike's symbiotic outreach to external stakeholders is a sense of urgency that the Earth's biosphere, on which all life and commerce depends, is threatened as never before by climate change and stressed ecosystems; and that it must help lead the way toward a more regenerative system. In doing so, it has adopted a strategy, much like Henkel's Factor-3, of making its products with more renewable materials and intellectual (design) content while reducing inputs of scarce resources and substances that harm Nature.

As stated in its year-end 2011 sustainable business report, its goal in advancing these practices is a world "where renewable sources of energy flourish, water is borrowed responsibly and returned clean to communities, waste is a new asset, workers across the industry are consistently valued and environmental impact will be a critical metric of success."[11]

We believe business has a critical role to play in meeting the challenges of a changing world—addressing climate change, preserving the earth's constrained resources, enhancing global economic opportunity—not by reducing growth but by redefining it.

Mark Parker, President and CEO, Nike[12]

---

11 Nike (2012, May 3). Nike's vision for a sustainable economy. Retrieved from http://extassets.nike.com/sponge_archives/2012/05/nikes_vision_for_a_sustainable.php.

12 Nike (2014, May 7). Nike's sustainability report shows company reducing environmental impact while continuing to grow. Retrieved from http://news.nike.com/news/nike-s-sustainability-report-shows-company-reducing-environmental-impact-while-continuing-to-grow.

Team building around learning

Understanding that fulfillment of Nike's outward-looking symbiotic goals depends on its inner capacity to learn and innovate, Mark Parker created inward-looking symbiotic goals toward making individuals and teams at Nike "faster, stronger, smarter." Given the enormity of the ecological, social, and economic challenges confronting Nike, his game plan was to "train for them" as a systemic whole rather than ad hoc constraints to be dealt with in the heat of competition.

His training strategy was to pose these challenges as a continuous "learning journey" to be met through personal quests for self-mastery and truth and through collaborative team thinking. To focus attention in constructive ways, employee teams in 2008 were asked to consider three core strategic questions:

- What new business concepts could enable Nike to thrive in a sustainable economy?

- How do we create a road map for evolving to a future state and solve the challenges preventing us from getting there?

- How do we continue to evolve and improve our current model during the transition?[13]

The power of these questions becomes apparent when you think of their focus. They center on learning (rather than finding fault), on matters of practical value (rather than abstract interest), and on hopeful images of the future (rather than maximizing profit). In each question the word "we" is used or implied to affirm that future strategy would arise from company-wide collaboration rather than

13   Nike (2009). *Corporate Responsibility Report 2007–2009*, p. 23. Retrieved from http://www.fibre2fashion.com/sustainability/pdf/nikesustainabilityreport.pdf.

executive retreat. The verbs used in framing them—"enable," "thrive," "create," "evolve," "improve," and "solve"—evoke an expansive view of alternative possibilities that is very different than the bottom-line-first vocabulary of industrial capitalism.

Beyond challenging employee teams to think holistically, Nike invited four institutional thinking partners to help it in its learning journey:

1. The World Economic Forum, an organization committed to "rethinking, redesigning and rebuilding" the global capitalist system

2. The Natural Step, a science-based authority on reducing corporate ecological impacts

3. Business for Social Responsibility, a resource on corporate best practices and cross-sector collaboration

4. Deloitte & Touche, a global authority on metric systems.

This gave employees access to a range of expert opinion as a means of broadening their perspectives.

To further collaborative dialogue among employee teams, Nike also created a multi-stakeholder forum of experts on labor, environment, community engagement, and sustainable reporting to assist in their training.

Considering all these elements, Nike's approach to learning was like an athlete preparing for competition: part individual effort, part teamwork, and part expert coaching. Its goal was to deepen the "bench" of employees capable of making smart, independent decisions and get work teams more engaged with suppliers in the creative process.

Toward decentralizing decision-making

A critical part of CEO Mark Parker's corporate training strategy was to decentralize decision-making, to enable Nike teams to respond more quickly to emerging challenges and opportunities. To do so, he accelerated an earlier five-year (2005–2009) program that looked to make the company flatter, simpler and more integrated.

By increasing the capacity of work teams to function independently, the company would increase its speed to market—a classic management by means (MBM) strategy. As described in its 2007–2009 corporate responsibility report, Nike put its reorganization process under the direction of a newly created sustainable business and innovation team. Comprised of its former corporate responsibility team plus its lean, energy, and compliance teams, this new team was intended to generate "a common understanding of Nike's corporate responsibility challenges, approaches and vision or aims ... realizing that the more integrated sustainable thinking is at the point of strategic intent, the greater the impact."[14]

As a later extension of this reorganization process, Nike introduced in 2012 a business simulation exercise where executive teams in diverse areas of the business—product development, finance, supply chain, and international—engaged in role playing. Called "NIKE2021," participants would take on the roles of CEO, CFO, and vice presidents of supply chain, product, brand, innovation, and sustainability. Then, using real-time data on challenges, such as global resource scarcities, the teams would compete in making strategic investments and partnerships while responding to macroeconomic events that impact the cost of materials and manufacturing, product availability, revenue and net income.

14   Ibid.

> We initially built NIKE INC 2021 to be played by 250 of NIKE, Inc.'s most senior leaders at the Corporate Leadership Team Meeting. Demand from leaders to scale the training to more NIKE INC leaders resulted in 17 follow-on events and 1,800 senior leaders experiencing the simulation. Tracking surveys show a massive shift in mindset and commitment to act to help NIKE respond to sustainability challenges and opportunities.
>
> Eric Hedaa, Nike Internal
> Communications Manager[15]

In another approach toward decentralizing decision-making, Nike launched in 2009 its "WE" portal, an online platform to help frontline employees and work teams connect with and contribute to social and environmental causes of their choosing. As described by a Stanford Business School case study, it was "an exercise in crowd sourcing ideas" where "employees would form teams and the winning ideas would be rewarded and acknowledged and, in some cases, applied to the business or funded for further development." In doing so, it allowed employees to engage higher levels of thinking and action while developing a "can do" team spirit.[16]

---

15   Eric Hedaa (n.d.). LinkedIn professional profile. Retrieved from https://www.linkedin.com/in/eric-hedaa-76b2732. Eric managed Nike's Sustainable Business and Innovation Team, which won the company's "Milestone Award" (2012) for "developing and launching NIKE INC 2021, an intense, 4-hour, multi-media business simulation aimed at driving a sustainability mindset shift and activating senior leaders to integrate sustainability into their strategies."

16   Jennifer Aaker, Ravdeep Chawla, & Sara Leslie (2010). NIKE WE: Design Meets Social Good. Stanford Graduate School of Business, Case M-328, p. 22.

In a similar spirit of decentralizing decision-making, Nike work teams began to share with suppliers in Asia and Latin America ideas and technologies developed by its Sustainable Business and Innovation Lab (part of Nike's renowned "Innovation Kitchen"). In one famous incident, Kasey Jarvis, a designer from the Innovation Kitchen, conceived a new shoe design after seeing heaps of discarded materials at a Nike factory near Ho Chi Minh City, Vietnam. This led to several years of experiments and supplier collaborations informed by Nike's newly minted "Considered design ethos," which favored using locally sourced materials plus energy- and water-saving manufacturing methods. The end result was Nike's famous line of "Trash Talk" shoes.

When introduced in 2008, Trash Talk shoes were an immediate hit. In 2009, they won "Best in Show" at the International Design Excellence Awards, and each year since, by popular demand, the line has been extended with fresh designs for multiple sports.

The Trash Talk story is important because it marks a further decentralization of decision-making at Nike. Calling their design methods an "ethos," Nike's design teams—now known as the Considered Group—made their knowledge and online tools available to all suppliers. This eventually led to numerous innovations utilizing recycled materials, including a line of national team uniforms for the 2010 World Cup soccer tournament in South Africa that were made entirely from recycled plastic bottles.

> Nike's Considered ethos challenges designers to use environmentally preferred materials, reduce waste, create sustainable manufacturing processes and use innovation to help reduce our overall environmental impact.
>
> Nike press release[17]

The Considered Group

The evolution of the Considered Group is another one of Nike's legendary stories. The name was conceived in 2005 with a new line of sustainable shoes, which its design team called "Considered." To team members, the name expressed their ideal of "considering what was right and doing what was right."[18]

Mark Parker, then serving as company president, quickly embraced the idea because he saw the design function as a key leverage point at the beginning of the value chain. Beyond that, the name captured the ideal of closing the loop—considering the impacts of choices over the entire life-cycle of a product from design through to end of life.

From the standpoint of decentralized decision-making, the Considered Group's philosophy (ethos) became a beacon to other work teams. As a creation hub, its spokes reached out to product

---

17 Nike (2008, February 13). Steve Nash and Nike turn garbage into "trash talk." Retrieved from http://news.nike.com/news/steve-nash-and-nike-turn-garbage-into-trash-talk.

18 Rebecca M. Henderson, Richard M. Locke, Christopher Lyddy, & Cate Reavis (2009). *Nike Considered: Getting Traction on Sustainability. MIT Sloan Teaching Innovation Resources*, p. 4. Retrieved from https://mitsloan.mit.edu/LearningEdge/CaseDocs/08.077.Nike%20Considered.Getting%20Traction%20on%20Sustainability.Locke.Henderson.pdf.

creation units, known as "triads," that included marketers, designers, and developers, who understood each product's technical details and coordinated their production with factories.

The group's primary decision-making tool, introduced in 2007, became known as the "Considered Index." This enabled product teams to quickly "score" designs based on the environmental impacts of materials used in production. As a catalog of environmentally preferred materials (EPMs) and bonding solvents, the index rated all materials on their energy use, greenhouse gas emissions, water use, land use, recycled content, recyclability, waste, and chemical use.

Later, in 2012, Nike added a materials sustainability index (MSI) that rates material vendors on compliance with a restricted substance list and a variety of other variables, including the quality of their environmental management systems.

Data collected on contract factory performance through MSIs and EPMs is today combined with other indexes that look to:

- Cost, quality, and on-time delivery

- Labor, health, and safety beyond compliance

- Country risk (political, social, economic infrastructure)

- Sustainability integration

- Innovation

Taken together, these give design teams a consistent framework to assess performance and a filter to make independent decisions.

> The Considered Group was at one and the same time a think tank, tool box, internal consultancy, competitive catalyst, the innovation end of sustainability, and an antenna to the outside world. Its mission was to serve as the hub of the Considered design ethos. ... The Index ran on an intranet calculator. Product teams could self-score their products in a minute by entering their product's BOM [bill of materials] number and clicking checkboxes for design and process options.
>
> MIT Sloan Teaching Innovation Resources[19]

One of the most revolutionary products to emerge from the Considered process is Nike's "Flyknit" racer shoe, introduced in 2012. According to *Fast Company* magazine, which named Nike the most innovative company of 2013, "What makes Flyknit so truly disruptive is that it isn't a shoe—it's a way to make shoes" that saves time, materials, energy, and cost.[20] Instead of cutting rolls of material into pieces, then stitching and assembling them, Flyknit technology knits the shoe's upper and tongue into a single integrated piece. Using only as much thread as needed in production, the shoe can be micro-engineered, even custom made, to improve durability and fit.

In terms of cost and environmental impact, Nike's Flyknit shoes reduce manufacturing waste by two-thirds compared with typical running shoes. In terms of performance, they are state of the art. Made with lightweight yet heavy-duty Vectran filaments designed for the U.S. space program, and created by knit threading rather

19   Ibid., pp. 6-9.
20   Austin Carr (2013, February 11). Nike: the no.1 most innovative company of 2013. *Fast Company*. Retrieved from http://www.fastcompany.com/most-innovative-companies/2013/nike.

than multiple layers of fabric, they are light and quick without sacrificing the support competitive athletes need.

As a further expression of the Considered ethos and Nike's symbiotic sense of purpose, the year after Flyknit was introduced it released an app called "MAKING" that shares with designers everywhere the contents of its vast MSI database. Accessible by cell phone, the database catalogs more than 75,000 materials, each scored on environmental impact and long-term sustainability. In this single gesture, Nike aroused the spiritual intelligence of its Considered Group by refocusing it on the health of the whole apparel ecosystem, and strengthened the reinforcing cycle of LAS that so energizes its employees and profits.

Looking beyond return on investment

As the Considered Group was being formed in 2006, Hannah Jones, then Vice President of Corporate Responsibility, called attention to the power of spiritual intelligence and the reinforcing cycle of LAS with a new metric called "ROI squared" (ROI^2). Her goal in creating this new notional metric was to reinforce the idea that corporate responsibility was intrinsic to a healthy business model, rather than being an irretrievable cost.

There were two elements to her value proposition—both of which affirmed the Considered ethos:

1. By designing out costs such as waste, Nike would become more efficient

2. By designing in qualities that buyers wanted, such as high-performance, ecologically desirable materials, Nike would gain market share

As the Trash Talk and Flyknit shoe lines ultimately proved, ROI^2 was a brilliant concept because it reinforced in everyone's mind the value of ecologically intelligent design. Looking back on Nike's success since ROI^2 was introduced, one has to be impressed. During the ten years between fiscal years 2006 and 2015, its return on invested capital grew from 20.42% to 26.29% while earnings per share tripled. Reflecting these results, Nike's stock returned roughly seven times the S&P 500 over that decade.

While cost savings on energy and materials obviously contributed to Nike's strong results during this period, the biggest factor was clearly the enthusiasm and spiritual intelligence of employees. As Austin Carr notes, the firm's employees "internalize" the value of their work, "vaulting Nike into the lofty heights of philosophical … corporate cultures alongside only Apple and Disney."[21] A Considered Group video on the Flyknit shoe distills the cachet: "This is not a shoe, it's an ethos … A shoe can't change the world, but an ethos can."[22]

A practical ethos

When it comes to the strategic importance of Nike's sustainability ethos, CEO Mark Parker doesn't mince words. In his 2011 letter to shareholders, he declared: "I believe that any company doing business today has two simple options: embrace sustainability as a core part of your growth strategy, or eventually stop growing."[23]

21   Ibid.
22   Retrieved from https://www.youtube.com/watch?v=1WuyE_x8Vs8.
23   Mike Parker (2011, July 13). Letter to shareholders. Retrieved from https://materials.proxyvote.com/Approved/654106/20110725/SHLTR_99556/images/Nike-Shareholder_Letter_2011.pdf.

In a 2015 Harvard Business Review interview, Chief Sustainability Officer Hannah Jones says this is true for two important reasons:

1. Because in a world of stressed ecosystems, sustainability has become a "key driver" in scenario planning

2. Because "consumers, particularly young consumers are increasingly prioritizing sustainability"[24]

However we approach it, Nike's sustainability ethos optimizes our only unlimited resource (human ingenuity) while conserving and stewarding the Earth's more finite resources.

That is not to say Nike has succeeded in closing the loop or that its learning journey is complete. Far from it. As the company is fond of saying, "There is no finish line."

The late Peter Drucker put it well: "Profit is like oxygen." Companies need it to stay alive. But it is not why they exist. Since corporate existence is premised on life, giving back to life becomes a necessary imperative—a sense of purpose above all others. That is the core principle of Nike's ethos. And it is the source of the company's extraordinary and continuing profits.

---

24 Hannah Jones (2015, April 16). Sustainable strides at Nike, Inc. *Harvard Business School Newsroom*. Retrieved from http://www.hbs.edu/news/articles/Pages/nike-sustainability-hbs.aspx.

7

Consciousness

Full-spectrum consciousness is the natural pathway to long-term success ... We found from our
research early on that full-spectrum organizations are the most successful.

Richard Barrett[1]

More and more it seems to me that this is what
a good culture means: the creation and maintenance of an environment in which everyone is
able to think clearly and creatively, to act ethically, and to air any issues or concerns absolutely
without fear.

David R. Morgan, CEO, Westpac Banking[2]

1   Richard Barrett (2006). *Building a Values-driven Organization: A Whole Sys-
     tem Approach to Cultural Transformation*. Oxford, UK: Butterworth Heine-
     mann, p. 57.
2   David Morgan (2004). Speech to the Trans Tasman Business Circle, April
     6, 2004, p. 3. Retrieved from https://www.westpac.com.au/docs/pdf/aw/ic/
     Trans_Tasman_Speech060404.pdf.

Like Nike, Australia's Westpac Banking Corporation got a wake-up call from its customers in the 1990s. Following a wave of branch closures and staff lay-offs while the bank was enjoying record profits, Westpac customers began complaining about the erosion of bank service. Although bank branches were replaced by automatic teller machines (ATMs), the lack of personal interaction left customers feeling that their personal needs were being dismissed and their communities abandoned. Because Australian banks had long portrayed themselves as utilities with a public service ethos, this incongruous move toward automation seemed both heartless and greedy.

To David Morgan, who became CEO in 1999, it was a moment of truth. With the loyalty and trust of communities, customers and staff eroding, he sensed the bank's license to operate was threatened. One of his first decisions, then, was to place a moratorium on branch closures and to introduce fee-free transactions for low-income customers and those on social security for whom the branches were a major convenience. As a longer-term solution, he converted each customer's home or business into an "electronic bank branch" via the internet, thereby enabling people and companies to obtain "user-friendly service 7 days a week, 24 hours a day."

Morgan's most important decision, however, was to instill a culture of consciousness and service that would broaden and deepen the bank's reach to customers. Speaking to an economic development group in August 2000, he presented his vision of this culture and how it would evolve: "[T]he future prospect for banks in Australia is not simply about how well we anticipate technological change, competition and globalisation but increasingly more about how well we operate within the social and environmental constructs applying across our industry."[3]

To attain that vision, Morgan espoused "a networked environment" where "employees are given the power to make real time decisions inside and outside of the company," where "the divide between management and labour" is eliminated and where managers become "responsible for teams that possess knowledge they do not possess themselves." Because of this, Westpac managers "do not direct, but facilitate, motivate and coach. It is a performance driven culture with strong vision and values, in which, ideally, staff explore the limits of creativity and inventiveness."[4]

In common with Ken Iverson's employee-centered growth strategy at Nucor, Morgan made it clear: "the staff are the bank ... the ones, substantially, who rebuild the threads of common understanding and trust with the community." Accordingly, they must be empowered "to draw their own conclusions about the worth of what we are doing ... Something like a virtuous circle applies ... It's a balancing act."[5]

Morgan's speech, which clearly recognizes the reinforcing cycle of living asset stewardship (LAS) and profit, describes in plain language how he sees it working for Westpac. His strategy was to make the bank more lifelike: more networked, self-organizing, open to feedback, symbiotic, and aware of changes in its operating environment. By further inspiring employees with a vision of becoming more socially and environmentally responsive, he created an organizational consciousness—an ability to see and sense the larger

---

3   David Morgan (2000). Speech to the Committee for Economic Development of Australia (CEDA) August 21, 2000, p. 2. Retrieved from http://www.westpac.com.au/docs/pdf/aw/ic/Brief_21Aug00_Morgan_CEDA.pdf.

4   Ibid., p. 9.

5   Ibid., p. 10.

systems of which they and the bank are a part—that turned Westpac into the sustainability and profit leader it is today.

The leverage points in this more holistic, integrative approach, as described throughout this book, are organically focused on people and Nature rather than mechanistically focused on capital. By engaging the hearts of employees—in effect, managing by means (MBM)—Westpac created a more durable process of generating profit. In theory and practice, it was a radical departure from the stereotypical bank approach of managing by results (MBR), which, in its obsession with bottom-line results, too often puts bank interests ahead of customers, society, and the biosphere.

Based on Westpac's results relative to its big bank peers, Morgan's strategy worked brilliantly. From the time he became CEO in 1999 through year-end 2015, Westpac's shares appreciated 265%—more than six times the return on JPMorgan Chase (JPM), the largest U.S. bank by assets—in spite of returning to shareholders as dividends a more generous portion of its earnings. Investor confidence in Westpac is further reflected via the premium investors are willing to pay for its shares relative to book value. At year-end 2015, Westpac stock traded at 1.8 times book value—64% higher than the 1.1 price/book ratio of JPM—and nearly triple those of industry giants Bank of America, Citigroup, Barclays, and Deutsche Bank, which hovered in the 0.50–0.75 range.

Westpac's record is even more impressive in the areas of sustainability and corporate ethics. Since 2002, when the global Dow Jones Sustainability Index was initiated, it has been named the world's most sustainable bank eight times. Since 2004, when the Global 100 Index of the world's most sustainable companies was launched, it has been included nine times, and it was rated first in 2014. Since 2007 when *Ethisphere*'s list of the "World's Most Ethical Companies" was introduced, it has been included seven times. In 2015, for the third consecutive year, Westpac was named as "Socially

Responsible Bank of the Year" in *Money Magazine*'s consumer finance awards.

This convergence of ethical management, sustainability leadership, and profitability makes perfect sense. Just as you would expect an inspired, consciously engaged individual to excel, the same holds for companies. In fact, Westpac's experience, like that of other companies profiled in this book, affirms that, the deeper companies go into life-mimicking cultures, the better their financial results are likely to be.

In spite of these now well-documented correlations, few of the world's top 50 banks take them seriously. Overcommitted to MBR, and motivated by bonuses tied to short-term results, they too often put returns on capital ahead of the very sources of their capital (people and Nature). This naturally exposes them to unnecessary risk. It also explains why so many had to be bailed out at public expense following the global financial crash of 2008.

Compared with the top-down, command-and-control cultures of most large banks, Morgan took the road less traveled. By cultivating a collaborative network of caring employees—rather than a small cadre of elite, bonus-driven traders and dealmakers—he fostered an organizational consciousness that looked to the whole of Westpac's business ecosystem. In doing so, he reduced Westpac's risk exposure and set it on its present course of profit and sustainability leadership.

Foundations of consciousness

Consciousness is a unique attribute of life. As described in this chapter, it encompasses a sense of selfhood, environmental awareness, values, ideals, and the ability to experience, relate, and feel, plus the capacity to envision a desirable future. In the context of corporations, it is an emergent property—one that becomes more developed as a firm becomes more lifelike in its organization and business practices.

David Morgan had an acute sense of these possibilities as he sought to make Westpac more responsive to its customers and communities. To sell the cultural changes he envisioned, he framed them in terms of returning the bank to its original values of individual and community service rather than as a disruptive overhaul of existing practices. In doing so, he often spoke of the bank's history: "Older than Australian democracy; older in fact than all but two Australian colonies," and how Westpac contributed "to the building of community and nation."[6]

This approach gave employees a sense that they were part of an important historic movement, one they could continually shape by thinking and acting with good conscience. It also appealed to their natural human instincts to connect, network, and serve, to do something meaningful with their lives.

A key part of Morgan's consciousness-building policy was to make ethics and corporate sustainability implicit qualities in the bank's culture rather than explicit directives handed down by executive edict. He approached this by appealing to employees' senses of "doing the right thing," keeping sight of "the common good" and making Westpac a "catalyst for multilateral collaboration" toward building social capital.

To reinforce the meme of Westpac as a leader of transformational change, he wrote in the bank's 2000 annual report:

6   David Morgan (2006). Speech to the Trans Tasman Business Circle, June 28, 2006, p. 3. Retrieved from https://www.westpac.com.au/docs/pdf/aw/ic/ DRM_TransTasman_060628.pdf.

> When the history of this period is written it won't only be
> about technological advances and ordinary people's mastery
> of that, it will be about the revolution in the way people work
> and how they relate to each other in the workplace.[7]

Morgan's appeal to the higher ideals of employees and their emotional intelligence had the desired effect on corporate morale. Based on annual surveys of employee engagement, Westpac's scores rose from a mediocre 56% in 2000 to a top-tier 71% in 2008, which was Morgan's final year as CEO. (For purposes of comparison the global norm for large financial companies at the time was around 65%.)

To bank analysts looking back on Morgan's tenure as CEO, he will, of course, be remembered for bringing Westpac to the front of its global peer group in terms of profitability. But the bank's returns on equity were only the tip of the iceberg. The much larger base of the structure, the part that too few analysts see, was the qualitative variable of culture—the shared beliefs, ideals, vision, and goals that make people want to think, learn, and commit.

Opening up to the system

To achieve Morgan's vision of a culture where people were able "to think clearly and creatively, to act ethically, and to air any issues or concerns absolutely without fear," he believed Westpac had to become more open in terms of information sharing, diversity of opinion, and empowering employees to make decisions in their fields of expertise. In essence, it had to break away from the big

7   Westpac (2000). *2000 Concise Annual Report*, p. 27. Retrieved from http://
www.westpac.com.au/docs/pdf/aw/ic/concise1.pdf.

bank stereotype of male-dominated hierarchies, where information and decision-making were restricted to a richly compensated few.

Accordingly, one of his first decisions was to create an open-book management system, where everyone in the company saw "some of the same information the board and executives saw."[8] Employees were provided with a series of "value maps"—learning tools to help them understand the bank's competitive environment, the importance of customer service, and the creation of shareholder value so they could better understand the system and their roles in it.

> When we initially canvassed the idea of using visual Learning Maps [our intent was] to give our people a better understanding of our business ... [By sharing] some of the same information the board and executives saw ... can now draw their own conclusions while gaining a better understanding of the background to the changes affecting them. In a way, all our staff get to sit in the big chair.
>
> Westpac, Annual Report, 2000[9]

The bank further opened itself up by treating staff like value-added partners entitled to enhanced benefits, extended parental leave, pay for performance, share ownership plans, flextime, and professional mentoring. As mentioned earlier, the role of leaders at every level was to serve employees' personal and career growth so staff, in turn, could better serve customers. To further staff development, Westpac also offered free online self-help courses and an

8   Ibid., p. 27.
9   Ibid., p. 27.

in-house academy with a leadership program focused on "behaviours necessary for success." The overarching purpose of all these activities was to imbue employees with the confidence that their knowledge and insights were important bank assets and that their conscientiousness mattered to group results.

One of Morgan's most important initiatives in opening up the bank's culture was a recruitment drive for working mothers, which he hoped would eventually increase their voice in senior management. Although he framed it in terms of creating a greater diversity of opinion and insight, he was clearly aware that the superior relational and listening skills of women would be an important part of the bank's outreach to customers and communities. As a result, "women in leadership positions" became a balanced scorecard objective and, importantly, a basis for executive compensation.

To attract women, Westpac made additional new offers: expanded child day-care centers, job share arrangements, merit-based selection processes, paid adoption leave, an information service that assisted employees in securing home help and health services, and a tax-effective option for paying childcare expenses out of salary. This naturally led to a rapid increase in the employment of women with children.

Within five years of introducing these incentives, women in management grew from 5% to 20%, and by year-end 2015 that ratio increased to 46%. During this time Gail Kelly, who succeeded Morgan as CEO from 2008 until 2014, became one of the world's most effective bank leaders. From 2009, her first full year as CEO, to year-end 2014, Westpac's net profit grew 119%—a result that was far ahead of leading banks in its money-center peer group (many of which still had seriously impaired balance sheets as a result of the 2008 global financial crash).

Ask only once

One of Morgan's most memorable early initiatives in making Westpac a more inclusive and conscientious culture was his "Ask only
once" program. Intended to remove bottlenecks that impeded customer service, it was a brilliant example of engaging employees in
creative problem-solving.

According to Westpac's 2002 annual report, the bank was receiving roughly 4,000 complaints a month from customers, 40% of
whom said they had to approach staff four or more times before
their issue was acknowledged or resolved, and it was clear to
Morgan that employees shared customers' frustration. As the
report noted, employees "want to help but many feel they lack the
tools and training they need."[10]

In making the case for corrective action, Westpac addressed employees' concerns in a context that looked to long-term outcomes:

> We could tell them they have to cope with the situation, but
> then we would lose some of our best people. We could say we
> have higher satisfaction ratings than most of our competi-
> tors, but, in truth, it's only by a small margin. We could say it
> doesn't really matter because we're still very profitable, but we
> could easily see our profits evaporate along with our reputa-
> tion if we did.[11]

By using employees' shared concern as a lever to brainstorm
ideas, and by sharing with them the big-picture trade-offs, "Ask
only once" took an inclusive bottom-up approach to solving the
problem rather than the more traditional one of top-down management directives. The goal was clear—"to solve problems at the first
point of contact … one call, one contact, and one solution." But

10 Westpac (2002). *2002 Concise Annual Report*, p. 2. Retrieved from https://
www.westpac.com.au/docs/pdf/aw/ic/2002_Concise_AR_FullFIN.pdf.
11 Ibid., p. 2.

more importantly, the means of making this plan happen were up for open discussion.

To further employee engagement in finding creative solutions, Morgan convinced his board to upgrade Westpac's employee share ownership plan by giving full- and part-time Australian staff annual free share distributions based on customer satisfaction and the bank's financial performance. It was a brilliant strategy. When employees could see how their customer service linked to bank profitability, and how profitability in turn linked to free share distributions, they responded with alacrity.

Building on staff ideas, the quality and efficiency of customer service took a significant jump, creating market share gains and a major improvement in the bank's expense/income (efficiency) ratio. During Morgan's tenure as CEO, that ratio improved from a mediocre 54% to a far more efficient 44.7%, enabling a greater portion of Westpac's earnings to drop to the bottom line. As a result, earnings per share began to grow faster than operating income, which ultimately led to an upgrade in the bank's credit rating from a strong Aa3 (Moody's) to an enviable Aa2.

Building on the spirit of employee engagement passed on to her, CEO Gail Kelly further improved Westpac's efficiency ratio to an impressive 41.6% by year-end 2014—significantly better than U.S. banks in its peer group, whose efficiency ratios, according to bankdata.com, averaged in the 61–65% range.

Toward full-spectrum consciousness

Westpac's ability to get the big-picture connection between ethical service and profitability, and its efforts to include employees in framing that picture, speaks volumes about its leadership. To advance this agenda, the year after Morgan became CEO, he created a new board-level Social Responsibility Committee focused on "total responsibility," including "best practice governance" and a "social accountability charter."[12] The following year Westpac signed the UN Global Compact and became one of the first global banks to issue a social impact report conforming to the triple bottom line standards of the Global Reporting Initiative (GRI). In quick succession, these decisive acts launched Westpac on its journey toward full-spectrum consciousness.

To Richard Barrett, who coined the term, full-spectrum consciousness occurs when organizations look beyond what they need to survive to their *spiritual* need for "internal cohesion, making a difference and service."[13] Because the social and biospheric world in which companies exist is in continuous flux, developing such consciousness necessarily requires a culture that is both systemically aware and committed to continuous learning.

In the course of building such awareness, Westpac's 2002 social impact report reflected on "the essential spirit of our company,"[14] including how "We must judge ourselves by how others see us, rather than how we see ourselves."[15] By addressing a broad spectrum of social, environmental, and economic concerns—developed in consultation with employees and other stakeholders—the report aimed to intensify the bank's concern for its ecosystem and its desire to live and work in harmony with that system.

---

12   Westpac (2003). *Who Cares? Our 2003 Social Impact Report*, pp. 8-10. Retrieved from https://www.westpac.com.au/content/dam/public/wbc/documents/pdf/aw/sustainability/2003_Social_Impact_Report.pdf.

13   Ideas for Leaders (2016). Using values-based leadership to drive performance. Retrieved from https://www.ideasforleaders.com/ideas/using-values-based-leadership-to-drive-performance.

14   Westpac (2002). *A Fresh Perspective: Our First Social Impact Report*, p. 37. Retrieved from http://www.westpac.com.au/docs/pdf/aw/sustainability/2002_Social_Impact_Report.pdf.

15   Ibid., p. 2.

> Our report is one of the first to conform to these new global standards that involve reporting on approximately 70 social, environmental and economic performance indicators … [W]e are seeking to acknowledge diverse stakeholder interests and to respond to their views on the role of corporations in charting a path to a healthy and sustainable future for our communities.
>
> David R. Morgan, CEO, Westpac Banking[16]

Barrett's theory, like Westpac's growth strategy, is grounded in the reinforcing cycle of LAS and profit. As he explains it, "Values-driven organizations have high levels of employee engagement; they generate higher earnings; they are more profitable, more customer focused, and more productive."[17]

This is corroborated by the consultancy Aon Hewitt, which notes a strong correlation between "best employer" engagement and stock market performance. In a 2014 survey it noted that top quartile companies "outperform the average company on revenue growth (6 percentage points), operating margin (4 percentage points) and total shareholder return (6 percentage points)."[18]

Based on the consultancy's five-year rolling analyses (2009–13), when top quartile global engagement scores were in the range of 72–6%, Westpac's scores ranged from 80% to 87%, suggesting it

---

16   Ibid., p. 3.

17   Richard Barrett (2013). *Unleashing Human Potential for Performance and Profit*, p. 1. Retrieved from http://www.valuescentre.com/sites/default/files/uploads/2013-08-05/Unleashing%20Human%20Potential%20for%20Performance%20and%20Profit.pdf.

18   Aon Hewitt (2014). *2014 Trends in Global Employee Engagement*, p. 9. Retrieved from http://www.aon.com/attachments/human-capital-consulting/2014-trends-in-global-employee-engagement-report.pdf.

was near the top of Aon's rating samples. During this time, when its largest bank peers were being bailed out at public expense, Westpac's shareholder returns were far in excess of its competitors.

Reflecting its balance sheet strength at the time, Westpac's credit rating (Aa2/P1) remained stable while those of its bigger Wall Street peers were downgraded. According to 2013 Moody's reports, JPM's rating (Aa3/P1) came closest, presumably reflecting its backing by the U.S. government, while those of Barclays and Deutsche Bank (A2/P1) were three rating points lower and those of Bank of America and Citigroup (Baa1/P2) were five points lower.

It is hard to argue with such numbers. Consciousness and success are linked in commerce as they are in Nature. As companies approach full-spectrum consciousness, they see more clearly how their economic performance depends on the biological web of life that is the source of all profit. And as they learn to better manage within the natural limits of this "commons," a virtuous cycle of improvement follows. This is especially true of banks, whose breadth of service reaches across the commons to customers in every sector.

Managing complexity

The more conscious companies become of the commons in which they operate, the better their capacities to manage complexity. One of CEO Gail Kelly's core strengths was her ability to see systems as a whole—the biological commons in which Westpac operated—and to convey that sensitivity and knowledge to employees.

Like Morgan, Kelly also had a talent for describing Westpac's evolving culture in simple language, often using metaphors as a way to describe how that culture functions. In her speeches and letters to shareholders we find a mind-set closely aligned to the iceberg meta-phor described in Chapter 1. Although her language and imagery are different—mental models are "soft wiring" and structures are "hard wiring"—she understood that soft wiring is the more impor-tant variable because it is the lens through which we see and sense the changing world around us. She calls it "the elephant in the room," an image of size and importance akin to the base of the metaphoric iceberg:

> At Westpac we talk … in terms of hard wiring and soft wiring. What do I mean by this? Well, hard wiring is the policies, the structures, the measures, the targets, the full on interventions that you need to drive a rigorous program. Soft wiring is … the story telling, the role modelling, the recognition systems, the cultural interventions, the calling out of behaviours and subtle biases. The elephants in the room.[19]

The "recognition systems" Kelly mentions encompass large sys-temic risks, such as:

- The hyper-leveraging of world financial markets that led to the 2008 global crash

- Increasing wealth disparities between the top and bottom of the economic pyramid

- The disruption of climate change, which threatens the very ground on which the pyramid sits

As she rightly suggests, banks that understand these risks to the commons, and manage them with prudent foresight, have advan-tages over those that don't.

---

19   Gail Kelly (2012). Speech to the AHRI/UN Women Australia Gender Equity in the Workplace Summit, July 24, 2012. Retrieved from http://www.genderequity.ahri.com.au/docs/ge_gail_kelly_speech.pdf.

Of course, managing complexity also means knowing where not to venture. Under Kelly, Westpac avoided trading in the hyper-leveraged global derivatives market with its layers of unknown counterparty risk. This set it apart from many big bank peers, which saw derivatives as a key profit center and, correspondingly, a source of executive bonuses. JPM, the most egregious example, had a visible derivatives book at year-end 2014 with a notional value of $65 trillion—roughly equivalent to world GDP and nearly *300 times its shareholder equity*. While managing this sum, no doubt, generates billions in revenues, it also makes the bank vulnerable because a fractional loss on that book, due to counterparty failure, could wipe out JPM's entire capital. By not playing in this risky venue, Westpac let its customers know that their interests come first.

We see similar behavior patterns in the more traditional venue of bank lending, where Westpac takes a longer-term relational approach while JPM focuses more on quick bottom-line returns. In consumer lending, for example, Westpac offers free counseling to people facing financial hardship with a goal of maintaining lasting relationships and strengthening the communities in which it operates. This contrasts with JPM's recent practice of selling mortgages to non-credit-worthy customers, which U.S. attorney Preet Bahrara called putting profits ahead of responsibility, then fraudulently selling these defective loans into government mortgage programs, and later repackaging them into mortgage-backed securities for sale to the public. While these practices generated quick fees (and management bonuses) for JPM, they contributed to the 2008 market crash and ultimately cost the bank $13 billion in legal and settlement expenses.[20]

---

20   Karen Freifeld, Aruna Viswanatha, & David Henry (2013, November 19). JPMorgan agrees $13 billion settlement with U.S. over bad mortgages. *Reuters*. Retrieved from http://www.reuters.com/article/us-jpmorgan -settlement-idUSBRE9AI0OA20131120.

Westpac's proactive approach to corporate and project finance is a further example of its skill in managing complex long-term risks. Reflecting its care for the biological and social commons into which it lends, Westpac looks beyond the financial stability of borrowers to their ethics and environmental, social, and governance (ESG) practices. In doing so, it recognizes that such considerations affect the health of its larger business ecosystem, which, in turn, underpins the health of its corporate borrowers. As a founding signatory (2002) of the Equator Principles on sustainable lending, Westpac is well known for its expertise in this area—a reputation that generates business across a number of asset classes including infrastructure for transportation, renewable energy, water, and environmental mitigation.

In all these circumstances, Westpac's ability to manage complexity originated in its soft wiring: its systemic awareness, its understanding of limits, and the engagement of employees at every level. When David Morgan retired as CEO in 2008, Gail Kelly's commitment to grow that soft wiring was likely a critical factor in her selection as his successor.

To Kelly's further credit, the year of her succession was when the global financial markets entered their worst crash since the Great Depression of the 1930s. Rather than being thrown off course, she led Westpac through the resulting turmoil by building on its core cultural strengths. As a result, during her six-year tenure as CEO, the bank's value more than doubled, from just under $50 billion to around $104 billion.

Defining success

It is hard to put a monetary value on Westpac's soft wiring under the conventions of traditional (linear) financial accounting. Yet it is clear that it does add value, albeit in a nonlinear way.

To put an exclamation point on this, consider Westpac's results in Gail Kelly's last year as CEO (2014). According to Marketwatch, its revenues and income per employee at year-end were $1,062,134 and $207,599 respectively. By contrast, those for the big Wall Street banks were significantly lower: JPM ($403,805 and $87,911); Citigroup ($390,166 and $29,892); Bank of America ($436,397 and $21,576); Deutsche Bank ($481,985 and $16,946); and Barclays ($245,223 and –$907).

The critical variable here is culture—the way biomimicry generates full-spectrum consciousness—which is hard to measure except in a very general way. As David Morgan once noted:

> In Westpac's case ... fully 70% of the value assigned to [its shares] by the market is not captured in the traditional financial measures. Employee commitment, occupational health and safety, workplace diversity, governance and leadership, customer satisfaction, product and service quality, brand strength, environmental impacts, the quality of relationships with stakeholders, and so on, are all critical to our longevity. But they currently have no place on a traditional P&L and balance sheet.[21]

Because there is no widely accepted formula for assessing the value of soft wiring, Westpac and other life-mimicking companies define their own criteria and metrics. As one might expect, these reflect the values they put on life (defined as the people, host

---

21 David Morgan (2006). Speech to the Trans Tasman Business Circle, June 28, 2006, p. 6. Retrieved from https://www.westpac.com.au/docs/pdf/aw/ic/DRM_TransTasman_060628.pdf.

communities, and ecosystems they serve and that, in turn, support them). Since such values influence the durability of long-term relationships and stakeholder trust, they are, as Morgan points out, critically important.

To aid in its ability to see systems as a whole, Westpac has developed over the years a balanced scorecard with key performance indicators (KPIs) relating to the quality of its forward-looking stakeholder relationships (relational equity) and how these correlate with its more conventional financial metrics. Today these come together in an integrated annual report as well as regular updates to its website.

When Morgan first introduced these KPIs, he had a catchy way of describing their higher purpose. He called it "managing *long*," managing *broad*," and "managing *ethically*."[22] Managing broad relates to the breadth of relationships captured by the KPIs, managing long relates to the connections between relational equity and long-term prosperity, and managing ethically draws attention to the role of ethics in sustaining long-term relationships. Thus, in three words, he described the importance of KPIs to Westpac's mission and future.

Today Westpac uses over 100 KPIs linked to its core strategy. Most of these track its ESG performance. All data and indicators are audited, independently verified, and published in its annual reports, which show five-year trends of its most important KPIs. Looking to the future, Westpac's reports also discuss material stakeholder issues revealed by its indicators, annual objectives on improving performance, and qualitative commentary by disinterested third parties on the materiality of disclosure.

---

22   Ibid., pp. 2-3.

> We see ESG management as ... a proxy for overall management quality, given the strong empirical correlation that has been shown with earnings quality. ESG metrics and ratings therefore can be used as an input into investor assessments of quality of management, in terms of risk management, operational performance, and value enhancement.
>
> Westpac, *Stakeholder Impact Report*, 2007[23]

Although these metrics lack the mathematic precision of algorithmic value at risk models that govern the behaviors of so many traditionally managed banks, they generally steer Westpac in the right directions.

One of the axioms of systems thinking is that it is better to be generally right than precisely wrong (as the highly leveraged Wall Street banks were in 2008). This is not to say that value at risk models are useless. Like a speedometer, they can tell us when we are going too fast. But they are insufficient for navigating and more complex decision-making, which require conscious engagement with the living world.

Breaking stereotypes

This chapter focuses on banking because it is at the very center of our global economic system: a venue where sound judgment, based

---

23   Westpac (2007). *2007 Stakeholder Impact Report*, p. 6. Retrieved from http://www.westpac.com.au/docs/pdf/aw/sustainability/2007_Stakeholder_Impact_Report.pdf.

on holistic thinking and a sense of systems limits, is utterly critical. Further, as an industry where corporations too often let their quest for money (capital) override their care for life (which is the ultimate source of their capital), it is ripe for reform.

Sadly, most of the world's large banks continue playing by the bottom-line-first rules of MBR. Beyond abetting industrial capitalist norms that have degraded the biosphere and society, their strategies also diminish their own financial returns.

Westpac is one of a small cohort of major banks that have broken away from this norm. Playing by a different set of rules centered on LAS, learning, and the development of organizational consciousness, it has generated far better financial results than banks that put profit first. Its MBM strategy recognizes that inspired, engaged people are the means by which corporations succeed, and that LAS is the means that inspires and engages them.

Key to that culture is a systemic awareness that Westpac is part of a larger biological and social commons that serves all life and future generations. An important premise of this approach is the elegantly circular (symbiotic) notion that living assets are the source of capital assets, in which case capital assets must, in turn, serve life.

Say what you will about LAS cultures and the soft wiring that enable them, they work brilliantly and get better as companies become more proficient at mimicking life—because that is the pathway to higher levels of consciousness. As Westpac approaches its 200th birthday, its commitment to LAS ensures that it will continue to evolve, thereby improving its chances of living another 200 years.

8

Toward industrial symbiosis

Collaborating in a symbiosis makes participant businesses stronger economically, and reduces consumption of resources.

Claus Søjle, Corporate Vice President, Novo Nordisk[1]

The symbiosis helps to make the Kalundborg refinery exceedingly energy-efficient, and it is the only oil refinery in the world where sulfur from the desulphurization facility is converted into liquid fertilizer.

Rasmus F. Wille, Managing Director, Statoil[2]

---

1   Quoted in Imagination for People (n.d.). Kalundborg industrial symbiosis. Retrieved from http://imaginationforpeople.org/en/project/kalundborg-industrial-symbiosis/.
2   Ibid.

The world's largest eco-industrial park, called the Kalundborg Symbiosis, is located in Denmark. Its three largest shareholder-owned corporate partners—Novo Nordisk, Statoil, and Novozymes (a Novo Nordisk spin-off)—are exemplary life-mimicking companies. Beyond being global profit leaders in their industries, they were for the year 2012 rated by Corporate Knights as first, third, and fourth among the world's "100 most sustainable companies." For the year 2015, all three were ranked in the top 50.

To understand how unusual this is, the top 100 are culled from a register of roughly 3,500 companies. That means less than 0.3% of global companies even make the list. The likelihood of three companies from the same small region making the Global 100 in the same year is even more remote. For that to happen with such regularity, the synergies and living asset stewardship (LAS) practices within the Kalundborg Symbiosis must be exceptional.

Like its constituent companies, the Kalundborg Symbiosis resembles the highly networked, self-regenerating, open culture of a natural ecosystem where resources are continually recycled within a closed loop. Started in 1961 as a water-sharing partnership between the municipality of Kalundborg and an oil refinery now owned by Statoil, the Symbiosis has evolved organically over more than 50 years into a model of how world commerce should operate in the decades ahead.

As in Nature, the evolution of Kalundborg has been entirely self-organizing based on the needs of each constituent and the availability of shared resources. At year-end 2015, its collaboration network consisted of 32 bilateral or trilateral commercial agreements centered on exchanges of energy (9 projects), recycling of waste products (11 projects), and recycling of water (12 projects). Having reached a critical mass of resource synergies and intellectual resources, it is now, like Silicon Valley, a magnet for innovative new enterprise.

Aside from Novo Nordisk, Novozymes, and Statoil, other prominent partners include:

- The state-owned 1,500 MW coal-fired Asnaes electric utility

- Gyproc, a wallboard company, part of the $44 billion global Saint-Gobain Group, which produces gypsum board from scrubbed Asnaes stack gas emissions

- Bioteknisk Jordrens, Northern Europe's market leader in bio-remediation

- Pyroneer, which converts biowaste into natural gas

- Noveren I/S, a waste handling cooperative of nine municipalities, which recycles household and industrial waste into power and heat

- Inbicon, an energy company that extracts biofuels from the agricultural wastes of nearby farms

- Kemira, a Finnish chemical company that buys sulfur extracted from Statoil's refining process and reprocesses it into sulfuric acid at a nearby plant

The commercial and ecological success of Kalundborg resides in thinking and acting as a coordinated group of partners rather than focusing only on individual efficiencies. Today it is a collaborative enterprise with an expanding group of profitable ventures—including local agriculture and fish farms—all drawing on the region's by-product and knowledge resources.

As a model of public–private partnership, the Symbiosis is a spectacular win–win. Facilities we normally think of as dirty, such as Statoil's refinery and DONG Energy's coal-fired utility, distribute their by-products in such a way that little effluent enters the environment. A network of nearby plants collects and harvests sulfur, fly ash, clinker, and waste heat for other commercial uses. Enzyme technologies developed at Novozymes convert biological wastes into fuels and high-value-added chemicals.

As these enterprises have flourished, new ventures and a world-class learning center have emerged within the Symbiosis, adding to its economic promise. The net result has been a stable, growing tax base, meaningful employment, lower utility costs (for water and energy), plus a cleaner healthier environment.[3]

The connections between the life-mimicking attributes of Kalundborg's three exchange-listed companies and their financial strengths are striking. Novo Nordisk, as we learned in Chapter 4, has long been a world profit leader in pharmaceuticals. Since de-merging from Novo Nordisk in November 2000, Novozymes (now the world leader in industrial biotechnology) increased shareholder value tenfold by year-end 2015. Statoil, which is 67% owned by the Norwegian government and operates in the more cyclical, slow-growth oil industry, grew its shareholder equity by 27% for the five years ending in 2015—a period during which the world price of oil declined 63% (from $99 to $37 per barrel).

Evolution of the symbiosis

In its early stages, development at Kalundborg (1961–81) centered mainly on sharing water plus untreated waste heat and refin-ery gas—a linear utility focus intended to economize on scarce resources. Since then it has evolved toward a more complex,

3   Robert J. Klee summarizes the Kalundborg Symbiosis in an "Eco-Industrial Development Primer" in Yale School of Forestry and Environmental Studies Bulletin Series (Bulletin 106. 2002). Retrieved from http://environment.yale.edu/publication-series/documents/downloads/0-9/106eip-cels_exercise1.pdf.

FIGURE 8.1   The Kalundborg Symbiosis

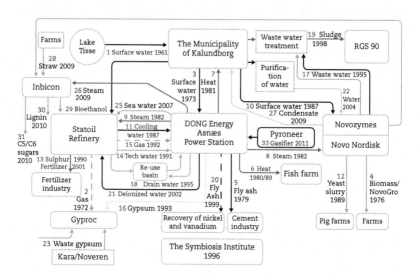

nonlinear design based on optimizing systems rather than compo-
nents. The term "symbiosis" affirms that the ecological, social, and
economic benefits of this approach transcend advantages to individual partners as they compound to benefit the whole community.

Figure 8.1 shows the circular multi-partnership structure of the
Symbiosis with a map of its resource exchanges within the system.
The dates shown on each waste-stream relate to the year those
resources were first harvested by symbiosis partners. The Symbiosis
Institute, founded in 1996, is its collective headquarters.

As the Symbiosis evolved beyond its initial utility exchanges
toward a more diverse circular economy, it increasingly used the
biological know-how of Novo Nordisk and Novozymes as important catalysts for new ventures. This is particularly evident in the
case of Inbicon (upper left corner of the diagram), which is today
the world's largest producer of second-generation bioethanol. By
harvesting three local waste-streams and selling its products to

three nearby companies, it has enriched its community and created new value in a resource-starved world.

It works like this: as a first step, Inbicon takes in 30,000 tons per year of low-value wheat straw supplied by local farmers—an agricultural by-product consisting of the dry stalks left after wheat grain removal. The straw then goes through a number of simple processing steps using waste steam from the Asnaes power station and enzymes from Novozymes. With these inputs, Inbicon produces on an annual basis:

- 5.4 million liters of bioethanol for the Statoil refinery

- 13,100 tons of lignin pellets for use as boiler fuel at Asnaes

- 11,200 tons of molasses for use as a livestock feed supplement

- Bio-nutrients that can be returned to farmers as fertilizer

Beyond the value added to its local partners and the Kalundborg community, Inbicon now licenses its patented technology to other bioethanol plants. The global market for this technology is immense because of its capacity to convert multiple types of biomass into valuable resources, with relatively little use of water and energy.

DONG (Danish Oil & Natural Gas), the 76% government-owned energy conglomerate that owns Inbicon, is a world leader in offshore wind energy and biomass conversion as well as Denmark's largest producer of electricity. To further diversify its sources of locally produced biofuels for its Asnaes power station, it has created the Kalundborg Integrated Energy Concept—a local partnership that leverages DONG's expertise in energy production and the knowledge of local biotech firms.

As part of this partnership, DONG leads a new venture called Cluster Biofuels Denmark, which seeks to transform additional waste-streams—municipal and industrial—into heat, power, chemicals, and other products that were formally derived from fossil fuels. One of its more promising R&D ventures uses micro-algae to clean waste-water while extracting from it biogas and other valuable resources.

As mentioned in Chapter 4, the biogas generator is part of a larger collaboration called the BIOPRO Development Center: a venture that also includes Novozymes, the Danish Technical University, the University of Copenhagen and a group of nearby biotech companies. Like Henkel's Factor-3, the purpose of this collaboration is to achieve factor efficiencies by generating more value with fewer inputs of virgin natural materials.

Adding to the intellectual resources of Kalundborg's business community, the Novo Nordisk Foundation supports the new BIOPRO World Talent Campus. Open to PhD-level students from around the world, it is committed to advancing the field of biotechnology manufacturing. As such knowledge accumulates within the community, it takes on a life of its own like other global innovation hot spots. With such resources available, it is no wonder that Novo Nordisk, Novozymes, Statoil, and DONG remain innovation leaders within their industries.

Although the headline story of Kalundborg today is its evolution as a world center of bio-innovation, it is important to remember where the Symbiosis started: as a venue for conserving water and energy. Because such conservation is a primary objective in virtually all the world's major economies, the Kalundborg model shows, at a minimum, what can be done via intelligent local collaboration.

Through the combined efforts of its community, Kalundborg now conserves 3 million m³ of water per year and has lowered its annual CO_2 emissions by 275,000 tonnes. For a small industrial city with a population of 16,300, that is no small achievement.

Considering these advantages in a world economy that uses up the resources of 1.6 planet Earths to provide the resources we use and to absorb our wastes, it is worth asking why the Kalundborg model is not more widely used.

> Moderate UN scenarios suggest that if current population and consumption trends continue, by the 2030s, we will need the equivalent of two Earths to support us. And of course, we only have one.
>
> Global Footprint Network[4]

The answer is that most efforts to replicate Kalundborg have started off the wrong way. Rather than evolving from the bottom up as organic, self-organizing, community-based ventures, too many planned symbiotic clusters have been engineered from the top down by governments in a hurry to get results. As a consequence, they become hampered by politically motivated agendas, linear command-and-control methods, and bureaucratic oversight (a topic we'll take up later).

Looking to the future, the effectiveness of the Kalundborg model is precisely its capacity to mimic the nonlinear (ecological, symbiotic) processes of Nature. When participating companies themselves do the same, we find a cohesive unity present in all natural systems—a fractal structure of networks within networks that organically develops from within.

Kalundborg's secret

The fractal structure of Kalundborg begins with individual networks in the community, which inform the internal and external

---

4   Global Footprint Network (2016). World footprint: do we fit on the planet? Retrieved from http://www.footprintnetwork.org/en/index.php/GFN/page/world_footprint/.

networks of resident companies plus scores of derivative networks through the Symbiosis Institute, university collaborations, company supply chains, and the like. From the individual (cellular) level to the systemic whole, we find in Kalundborg's rich variety of networks shared symbiotic interests and a universal commitment to the health of the commons—qualities that facilitate communications as well as the sharing and exchanges of resources.

From its beginning as a community utility to share water and energy, the Symbiosis has taken its member companies to higher levels of LAS by leveraging local knowledge and resource exchanges while also serving as a global learning center through its collaborative BIOPRO World Talent Campus.

The feedback effects of such knowledge sharing and experimentation naturally increase the effectiveness of all members plus the community as a whole. When DONG Energy formed the biomass-to-energy companies Inbicon and Cluster Biofuels Denmark, it did so in partnership with nearby companies, which saw in each venture benefits to themselves and to the community. The cohesiveness of those shared interests gave all companies involved a stable platform on which to grow and prosper.

Kalundborg was in many ways the ideal location to start such ventures because it is a small tight-knit community where the participating companies are located within a few kilometers of one another. Early resource sharing was accelerated by the formation of the Environment Club—a precursor to the Symbiosis Institute—where local businessmen could regularly meet to exchange ideas and find new synergies.

In addition to this geographic proximity, there was also an "ideological proximity" of shared values. Consider the Novo Nordisk Foundation (founded in 1951), which owns through its Novo A/S subsidiary a majority of voting shares in Novo Nordisk and Novozymes. The open commitments of both companies to advance the triple bottom line of ecological, economic, and social progress, supported by their biotechnology skills, have enabled other companies in the Kalundborg community to leverage their symbiotic practices.

According to its charter, the foundation has two life-affirming objectives: "To provide a stable basis for the commercial and research activities conducted by the companies within the Novo Group and to support scientific and humanitarian purposes."[5] From its earliest interests in advancing human health, the foundation has diversified strongly toward advancing systemic health—particularly in response to the challenges of ecological overshoot and climate change.

Today this commitment to systemic health is expressed through the foundation's Center for Biosustainability. In its aim to catalyze "sustainable bio-based industry," the center challenges a foundational premise of the industrial capitalist model, whose operating leverage is largely based on carbon-emitting fossil fuels.

The Foundation uses its independence, flexibility and long-term perspective to promote world-class research [and] address the pressing challenges of the future—to benefit both individuals and society as a whole.

Novo Nordisk Foundation, vision statement[6]

Like the open-source information on Unilever's Open Innovation Portal, Nike's MAKING app and Henkel's alternatives to animal

5   Novo Nordisk Foundation (2016). What is the Foundation? Retrieved from http://novonordiskfonden.dk/en/content/charter.

6   Novo Nordisk Foundation (2016). Vision and mission. Retrieved from http://www.novonordiskfonden.dk/en/content/vision-and-mission.

testing, the Kalundborg Symbiosis, abetted by the Novo Nordisk Foundation, looks to the health of the global commons on which all companies, and indeed all life, depend.

The energy that sustains this open sharing, as we have seen throughout this book, resides in the complex neurology that connects our hearts and brains. When engaged and synchronized with our biophilic gut instincts, this activates our highest spiritual intelligence. Fortunately, there is no shortage of this intelligence. It exists worldwide in all cultures as an expression of humanity's inbred life-affirming instincts. Although suppressed by top-down governance structures, it is a powerful lever for transformative change when allowed to operate in life-mimicking organizations— a topic we will take up in the next chapter.

Failed attempts to replicate Kalundborg

Governments everywhere would naturally like to achieve Kalundborg's results. However, when they try to do so via command-and-control processes they subvert the organic, self-organizing processes that have made Kalundborg a success.

This largely explains the failures of U.S. efforts to create ecological investment parks. Initiated by the U.S. President's Council on Sustainable Development, these efforts lacked the spontaneous local cohesion of Kalundborg because they were created with politically motivated national agendas, such as brownfield redevelopment, economic rehabilitation of depressed areas, and outright vote buying. The willingness of corporations to participate in such ventures was further complicated by concerns about bureaucratic oversight by diverse agencies, including the Environmental Protection Agency, Department of Energy, Department of Labor, and the Department of Justice. Thus, rather than making it easy for constituent companies to move ahead with symbiotic exchanges, this approach constrained progress with red tape and restrictive agendas.

In a frequently cited article on the failure of ecological investment parks and other centrally planned clusters, Yale professor Marian Chertow explained in the *Journal of Industrial Ecology* why government attempts to plan eco-industrial parks "from scratch ... have rarely come to fruition in a sustainable way." If governments desire to play a role, Chertow says, it should be to "steer" approaches to resource sharing in "geographically related areas by choosing projects with demonstrable kernels of self-organization that can emerge more fully as viable industrial ecosystems."[7] In other words, facilitate but otherwise stay out of the way.

Looking back over the half-century since the Kalundborg experiment started, that is precisely what the government of Denmark and municipal authorities did. Rather than trying to control the development of the Symbiosis, they steered its evolution by acting as a partner in the sharing of water and waste industrial heat (the municipality) and by speeding regulatory approvals (Danish Environment Ministry). On no occasion did they try to control the process.

Table 8.1 summarizes the critical differences between these two approaches to industrial symbiosis. In it we find that the same six attributes used to define companies that mimic life also apply to symbioses.

Reading down from the top of the table, we begin to see how these systemic differences affect different outcomes and why the ecocentric Kalundborg model today remains the standard of excellence.

---

7   Marian R. Chertow (2007). "Uncovering" industrial symbiosis. *Journal of Industrial Ecology, 11*(1), 11-30 (p. 26). Retrieved from http://is4ie.org/resources/Documents/uncovering%20IE.pdf.

TABLE 8.1   Contrasting approaches to industrial symbiosis

Attribute	Traditional model	Ecocentric model
Organization/ structure	• Highly centralized • Hierarchical structure	• Decentralized, localized, diverse • Deeply networked
Culture	• Top-down, command/ control • Concerned with authority • Tied to political agendas • Focus on quick results	• Bottom-up, self-organizing • Concerned with real solutions • Bilateral exchanges of value • Focus on slower organic change
Behavior	• Quest for economic advantage • Desire to look successful • Impatient, reactive	• Quest for harmony, insight, stability • Desire to collaborate, learn, adapt • Patient, reflective
Openness to learning	• Closed system, set agenda • Rule-bound thinking • Single-loop learning process	• Open system, experimental • Continually looking for new ways • Double-loop learning process
Goals	• Serving political constituents • Economic growth • Power	• Serving all life (people and Nature) • Economic resilience • Adaptive capacity
Consciousness	• Narrow spectrum, utilitarian • Linear thinking • Self-centered • Reductionist, deterministic	• Broad spectrum, values-driven • Systems (nonlinear) thinking • Holistic, symbiotic • Continually evolving

Can governments advance industrial symbioses?

If local self-organization is a prerequisite for success in creating durable industrial symbioses, as Chertow suggests, we are left with the question: is there anything governments can do to speed the development of these systems, which are so obviously needed today?

The answer is "yes," but only if governments are willing to be facilitators rather than central planners. In a widely cited 1998 *Harvard Business Review* article, Michael Porter says "the appropriate policy towards cluster development is usually to build on existing or emerging areas that have passed a market test."[8] To achieve optimum effectiveness, government involvement should therefore be limited to zoning, permitting, research partnerships, planning assistance, and other pump-priming initiatives.

Since Porter's article, limited government involvement has become a standard for successful symbioses. Two prominent examples of this standard are the Kwinana Industries Synergies Project (KISP) in Western Australia, founded in 2001, and the symbiosis at the port of Moerdijk in Holland, started in 2007. In both cases, the impetus for symbiotic collaboration came from the bottom up by local companies with governments acting as partners or facilitators rather than as central planners.

Australia's KISP grew out of the Kwinana Industries Council, a self-organized group of large mineral processing companies and a utility that formed in 1991. In collaboration with Curtin University of Technology, KISP's goals generally reflected those of Kalundborg:

- Convert waste-streams into value-added resources for other manufacturers

---

8   Michael E. Porter (1998). Clusters and the new economics of competition. *Harvard Business Review*, Nov–Dec.

- Reduce greenhouse gases via improved energy efficiencies

- Reduce the use of fresh water by reprocessing waste-water

One of the early partners in these KISP projects was the state-owned energy company, Western Power, which sold superheated steam to a local pigment manufacturer. Another innovative project, which required state licensing, was the development of a wetland planted with sedges to incorporate various biological processes that reduce nitrogen waste-streams. As KISP's success and promise grew, it later received research funding from the Australian Commonwealth Cooperative Research Centre and the Western Trade Coast Industries Committee, both of which included representatives of local governments.[9]

With that funding, KISP developed a customized input and output database to track material flows with the objective of identifying new synergies and setting development priorities to further close the loop. One of the database's top priorities was to expand from Kwinana's initial "utility synergies"—focused mainly on reducing water and energy flows within the park—toward a wider variety of vertical "by-product synergies," such as those found at Kalundborg.

Although much younger than Kalundborg and lacking the diversity of its stakeholders, Kwinana has produced impressive results. In a May 2010 report, the Kwinana Industries Council reported the symbiosis achieved:

- Some 32 by-product and 15 utility synergies

- Water savings of 8,200 gigaliters/year

9   Albena Bossilkov, Dick van Beers, & Rene van Berkel (2005). Industrial symbiosis as an integrative business practice in the Kwinana Industrial Area: lessons learnt and ways forward. Retrieved from http://www.docin.com/p-310390901.html.

- Energy savings of 3,750 trillion joules/year

- Waste reductions of 421,600 tonnes/year

- Gas emission reductions of more than 134,000 tonnes/year

- CO_2 emission reductions equivalent to removing 73,000 cars from the road[10]

The newer symbiosis at Holland's Moerdijk port started as a pilot project among local industries following discussions with its port authority about developing an environmental monitoring and management system. One of the first priorities of the pilot was to create an energy web where companies would mutually exchange heat, steam, and CO_2—the design of which was partially funded by a grant from the Province of North Brabant. As planning dialogue progressed, a coordinating committee of companies was established in 2009 to create a "knowledge platform" for exploring new ideas on working conditions, the environment, and safety.

In 2010, during the course of Moerdijk's pilot project, a "front-runners" group was formed of companies with "visible sustainability efforts" to inspire others toward integrative action. To become a front-runner, companies had to conduct a self-assessment on five criteria:

1. Good governance

2. Working conditions

3. Environmental impact

4. Social commitment

5. Fair conduct of business

---

10   Kwinana Industries Council (2010). *Industry's Environmental Synergies*, p. 3. Retrieved from http://www.kic.org.au/environment/synergies.html (follow link for "Existing Synergy Examples").

These self-assessments were later audited by an accreditation committee under the aegis of the Ecoports Foundation and other independent experts in the field of sustainability.[11]

Although sketchy in places due to a lack of data comparability, the audit revealed significant progress. Between 2007 and 2010—a time when the total number of shipping tons handled by the report increased by 32%—the symbiosis reportedly achieved significant declines in net electricity consumption (34%), industrial water usage (28%), air quality complaints (29%), and direct discharges into the sewer system (7%). Between 2008 and 2010 it also reduced hazardous wastes by 25%. For the year 2010, 73% of nonhazardous wastes generated at the symbiosis were reused or recovered with an additional 10% allocated to a waste incineration plant to generate energy.[12] The only fallback reported during the 2007–10 period was an increase in air emissions (mostly CO_2), presumably due to the increase in tonnage shipped through the port.

Now engaged in a five-year plan (2011–15) to create a "multicore loop system" for the "beneficial use of energy/heat, water and residual currents," Moerdijk's symbiosis is exploring ways to decouple economic growth with ecological and social impacts.[13] To accomplish this, ten study groups and multi-stakeholder committees were established to assess potential by-product synergies. The government's primary role was limited to facilitating collaboration and raising appropriate questions that needed to be addressed, such as performance indicators, water management, public safety, and noise abatement. In addition, a system of "opportunity boards"

---

11   Port of Moerdijk (2012). *Port Environmental Review System, July 2012*. Retrieved   from   http://www.havenschapmoerdijk.nl/media/1221/pers_document_2012_def_definitief.pdf.

12   Ibid., pp. 29-38.

13   Ibid., p. 6.

was established that listed opportunities for companies at the industrial park to reuse each other's waste materials.

The Port Authority that oversees Moerdijk's symbiosis has a small staff that takes pride in working efficiently. As stated in its brochure, "lines are short and, where needed, immediate action can be undertaken—both for companies and authorities." By means of cooperation within and between government bodies, decisions are made without conflicting regulations. To simplify environmental permitting, local and port authority governments have created an "all-in-one" filing (*omgevingsvergunning*) that can be submitted digitally, replacing an earlier system where 25 licenses and permits were required in the fields of environment, building, and zoning. Consequently, "There is one appeals procedure and one control body responsible for coordinating supervision and enforcement."[14]

Although it is difficult for governments to resist centrally planned economic solutions, the projects at Kwinana and Moerdijk affirm that the light-touch approach of Kalundborg is the most effective path toward achieving symbiosis. As in Nature, symbiosis works by self-organizing, bottom-up collaboration rather than imposed top-down control. If governments want to create more industrial symbioses, this is the path they must take.

Reinventing capitalism

The success of Kalundborg, like that of the seven companies profiled in this book, presents a new and vastly improved form of capitalism. As such, it is a reinvention—not an overthrow.

14   Ibid., p. 39.

Unlike the dying remnants of traditional capitalism, which today rely on government financial and regulatory support, this new breed of capitalism is self-sustaining and financially sound. As evidence we have the balance sheet strength of companies in the Global LAMP Index® and Focus Group (Appendix 3), and the economic miracle of Kalundborg.

The fallacy of the older industrial capitalist model, as revealed in Chapter 1's iceberg diagrams, is its preoccupation with *quantitative* data, such as GDP, profit, and per capita incomes. This mind-set reflects a belief that the more technology and capital humanity can bring to bear on Nature, the more we will be able to consume and the better off we will be.

However tempting this worldview may be, it contains two glaring oversights:

1. Infinite GDP growth is impossible on a planet with finite resources

2. Valuing capital assets more than living assets makes no sense because people and Nature are the source of capital assets

By contrast, ecocentric capitalism looks at the world primarily in the *qualitative* terms of systemic health, the evolution of knowledge, and humanity's capacity to adapt with the rest of life. It is founded on a fundamental belief that if we do these things in ways that serve Nature as well as society, profit will take care of itself— just as a healthy ecosystem continually renews itself by producing surplus nutrients.

The concept of LAS goes a step further. Stewardship implies care and responsible management rather than absolute ownership. It is a moral responsibility grounded in the Golden Rule. For this reason, the true meaning of LAS is *respect for life*.

Although that is a foreign concept in the world of traditional capitalism, it is the way the real (natural) world works. If our goal is to live and work in harmony with the living world and prosper with it—rather than deplete it and suffer the consequences—we must behave as it does. This is the only viable way forward.

9

The emerging corporate renaissance

Rewiring homo economicus, that's what it is about.

Ernst Ligteringen, CEO,
Global Reporting Initiative[1]

On a finite planet, where all life (including human life) is dependent on finely tuned ecosystems, unending physical growth is categorically impossible. However, the quest for human development, happiness, and well-being presents limitless possibilities.

Alan AtKisson[2]

1   Quoted in KPMG Advisory NV (2010). *Integrated Reporting: Closing the Loop of Strategy*, p. 7. Retrieved from http://www.kpmg.com/UA/en/IssuesAndInsights/ArticlesPublications/Documents/Integrated-Reporting.pdf.
2   Alan AtKisson (2012). *Life Beyond Growth*. Retrieved from http://donellameadows.org/archives/life-beyond-growth/.

Relative to the span of life on Earth, humanity is a young species. Evidence of anatomically modern humans goes back roughly 200,000 years—about 0.01% of the time mammals have inhabited the planet and a far smaller fraction (0.003%) of the time since simple animals first appeared.

To say we are still learning and adapting as a species is an understatement. Since the agricultural revolution 12,000 years ago, humanity's accumulation of knowledge has been accelerating as we build out from a growing base of shared information. Important milestones include the invention of cuneiform writing 5,200 years ago, the development of deductive (Greek) mathematics 2,700 years ago, movable type printing (Han Chinese) 1,000 years ago, Newtonian mechanics 400 years ago, Farraday's electricity-producing dynamo 200 years ago, and now the profusion of modern sciences, such as quantum theory, ecology, system dynamics, and cognition, which have given us new insights into our relationships with the whole of life.

In the course of these discoveries, our relationships to each other and Nature have been through some wide pendulum swings. In the earliest days of human civilization, survival was based on collaborative behavior and living in harmony with the natural world. However, as our accumulation of knowledge and technology grew, we began to think of ourselves as separate from and above Nature—a movement that reached its apotheosis during the Industrial Revolution. Today, with world population growth straining the resources of an ecologically stressed planet and faced with the reality of life-altering climate change, we are experiencing a rebirth of interest in returning to older ways of living in harmony with each other and with Nature. Like any species under threat, we are trying to learn and adapt.

In the Introduction, we compared the emerging renaissance in human consciousness, now playing out in companies that mimic life, to the earlier European Renaissance of the 14th–17th centuries. The impetus to change in that earlier period arose from feudal repression, poverty, filth, and plague—threats to human wellbeing. The impetus to change today, however, is a far more serious threat to the entire biospheric web of life on which we humans, and all species, ultimately depend.

Our adaptive responses to these conditions reflect powerful shifts in human consciousness. During the European Renaissance, it was one of self-discovery—characterized by anthropocentric humanism —in which we learned we could be masters of our own lives without having to mediate through the Church or corrupt medieval power structures.

Such ideas were powerfully expressed in the 17th-century writings of Sir Francis Bacon and René Descartes, who anticipated the Industrial Revolution by pronouncing humanity's "right" to dominion over Nature "which belongs to it by divine bequest" (Bacon), and by asserting that we could become "masters and possessors of Nature" through "science and rational thought" (Descartes).

Today's emerging renaissance, by contrast, looks on humanity not as a master or possessor of Nature, but as an integral part of it: a highly evolved species that is now learning to think systemically and live harmoniously within the biospheric web of life. Moved by a conscious acceptance of our interdependence with the rest of life, this emerging new worldview is both holistic and ecocentric.

From ego to eco

Otto Scharmer, cofounder of the innovative Presencing Institute and U.Lab at MIT, speaks brilliantly for this new worldview. He frames it in terms of discovering and cultivating the social field in which we live—defined by our relationships with the emerging "whole" of biosphere and society.

Commenting on that social field, he says what most of us know in our hearts:

> Today, in most social systems, *we collectively produce results that no one wants.* These results show up in the form of environmental, social, and cultural destruction. The ecological divide (which disconnects self from nature), the social divide (which disconnects self from other), and the spiritual divide (which disconnects self from self) shape the larger context in every large system change today.[3]

The "disconnects" to which Scharmer refers arise from habits and learned behaviors that spread from the anthropocentric (*ego-centered*) worldview of the 17th century into industrial capitalism. By putting capital ahead of living assets (people and Nature), this mind-set contravened the defining attribute of the Earth, which is life itself, and set us on a self-destructive path.

In his work at the Presencing Institute and at MIT's U.Lab, Scharmer aims to reconnect us to the *eco-centered* world that is both source and sustenance to all humanity. Founded to advance the skills of adaptive learning, the institute and lab seek to expand human consciousness toward shared visions of the future. The word "presencing" describes their approach: an amalgam of the word "sense" (feeling future possibilities) and "present" (the state of being in the present moment), it asks participants to suspend habitual thinking patterns and open their senses to emerging new possibilities.

---

3   Otto Scharmer (2015, June 6). The blind spot: uncovering the grammar of the social field. *Huffington Post.* Retrieved from http://www.huffingtonpost.com/ otto-scharmer/uncovering-the-grammar-of-the-social-field_b_7524910. html.

In doing so, presencing utilizes the powerful heart–brain neurology that is the source of our higher awareness and spiritual intelligence. As an ecocentric visioning process, it looks to engage people from diverse backgrounds and professions through processes of deep, empathic listening that enable the group to see beyond habitual boundaries. As Scharmer says: "The actual process has a lot to do with paying attention, opening up your awareness, going to the edges of the system and of yourself, and creating a space where we can venture with each other in a safe, exploratory way."[4]

> To establish this deep innovation process within and across institutions, leaders need a new social technology that allows them to tune three instruments: the Open Mind (IQ); the Open Heart (EQ or emotional intelligence); and the Open Will (SQ or spiritual or self-intelligence).
>
> Otto Scharmer[5]

Scharmer's process of engagement aims to catalyze and accelerate the emerging global renaissance from egocentric capitalism toward a new ecocentric system of stewarding the shared ecological and social commons that is the ultimate source of life and profit.

4   Peter Senge, Otto Scharmer, & Darcy Winslow (2013). 30 years of building learning communities: a dialogue with Peter Senge, Otto Scharmer and Darcy Winslow. *Reflections, The SoL Journal on Knowledge, Learning and Change*, 12(4), 40-52 (p. 49). Retrieved from https://www.presencing.com/sites/default/files/page-files/Senge_Scharmer_Winslow_Vol12.pdf.

5   Otto Scharmer (2010). The blind spot of institutional leadership: how to create deep innovation through moving from egosystem to ecosystem awareness. Paper prepared for the World Economic Forum, Tianjin, China. Retrieved from http://www.ottoscharmer.com/sites/default/files/2010_DeepInnovation_Tianjin.pdf.

Conceptually, it is a switch from bottom-line-first to "life-first" thinking within the scope of commercial enterprise. Although foreign to textbook economics and traditional business practices, Scharmer's U-process is today used by some of the world's most profitable companies, including Unilever, Nike, and Google.

In common with living asset stewardship (LAS), the U-process is clear about the centrality of the human heart in "sensing" a new way forward. As a method of group dialogue, it asks us to pass through an "inner gate" where we "let go" of our ego, which is driven by perceived special interests of the moment, and "let come" our more spiritual self—a process where we open our heart, mind and will to the "emerging whole" that connects us to the larger web of life. To Scharmer, this "power of … intention creates an energy field that attracts people, opportunities, and resources that make things happen."[6] Framed as such, it is a means of moving organizations toward higher levels of LAS, where people engage their hearts as well as their minds in creating a more sustainable future.

Scharmer's great insight is all the more important because it comes at a time when humanity has pushed the Earth's ecosystems beyond their natural carrying capacities. Consequently, our need to see and sense systems as a whole is more important than it has ever been in history.

In business, the more developed this sensing capacity becomes, as companies evolve toward LAS cultures, the better they become in forging strong relationships with the employees, customers, partners, and investors who support their commerce.

6   Otto Scharmer (n.d.). Executive summaries. Retrieved from http://www. ottoscharmer.com/publications/executive-summaries.

Importance of life-affirming cultures

Peter Drucker once remarked that: "Culture eats strategy for breakfast." Although this was a general observation, not one about Scharmer's U-process or LAS, it is certainly affirmed by the case studies of our seven corporate exemplars.

Companies that practice LAS are acutely aware of the centrality of life; and the U-process heightens that awareness. Both practices are cultural leanings that arise from the heart rather than strategic ones that emanate from the brain. Yet both also have strategic value because they enable companies to engage stakeholders from a common reference point. This gives life-affirming companies a coherence that magnifies their creative energy.

Figure 9.1 summarizes how such life-centered cultures work. What we see here is a web of **mutually reinforcing relationships** that grow stronger as the system becomes more coordinated and harmonic. There is nothing linear about it—no shortest path to the bottom line. The emphasis, instead, is on nonlinear reinforcing feedbacks that coalesce to strengthen the system.

This diagram affirms that the more competently companies mimic life in their visions, missions, and values, the stronger their relationships with key stakeholders are likely to become. The strength of those relationships comprises a firm's "relational equity." It is the best leading indicator of financial equity we know because it forges bonds of constructive feedback and loyalty that cultivate market share and profitability.

The effectiveness of relational equity as a leading indicator of financial equity is evident in the shareholder returns of the seven LAS exemplars described in this book (our Focus Group) relative to the Global LAMP Index® from which they were drawn and the benchmark MSCI and FTSE world indices, which are their most relevant comparators.

FIGURE 9.1   **The LAS model**

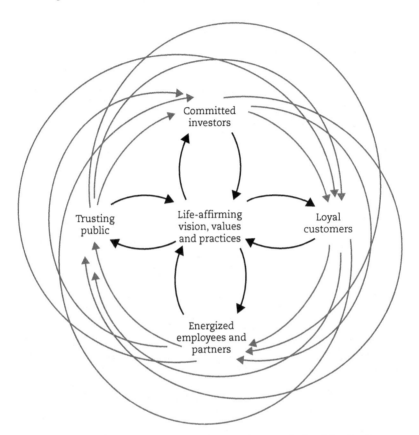

This diagram describes a firm's essential constituent relationships. In the center we see how each one, inspired by the firm's core vision, values, and practices, engages in a continual exchange of value. The outer rings describe feedback channels between constituents, which reinforce their trust and loyalty to the firm. For example, inspired employees build public trust, which reinforces commitments to the firm by investors, customers, and partners. Loyal customers and committed investors, in turn, validate the firm to all constituent groups. In these ways, each constituent builds on the enthusiasm of others, opening channels of communication and value exchange.

The conceptual design of the LAS model and its feedback effects was created in collaboration with Richard Karash.

As revealed in Table 0.1 in the Introduction, since the start of the millennium on January 1, 2000, the compound annual growth of shareholder returns of the Focus Group was eight times higher than the MSCI World Index and seven times higher than the FTSE World Index. The larger Global LAMP Index® also significantly outperformed those benchmarks, although its excess return was less because the average LAS virtuosity of its 60 constituents was below that of the Focus Group.

These findings strongly support the notion of an emerging corporate renaissance in business practice. The common threads of this awakening are:

- Our growing capacity to sense and act on nonlinear eco-centric feedback from the living world around us

- Our rejection of the excesses of industrial capitalism and consumerism

A fundamental insight of this renaissance is that living assets (people and Nature) have greater value than nonliving (capital) assets—the virtual opposite of industrial capitalist thinking. Like "cracking the code of life" (DNA) in 1968, the emerging renaissance of LAS has opened vast new vistas of human awareness and innovation.

We see in the previous chapters evidence of this emergence expressed in so many ways:

- In the work of the Novo Nordisk Foundation's Center for Biosustainability, which aims to catalyze "sustainable bio-based industry" (as an alternative to the carbon-based industries that launched the Industrial Revolution)

- In United Technologies' quest to decarbonize urban life and intercity air travel

- In Henkel's quest for Factor-3 and Factor-5 efficiencies through which it seeks to produce ever-higher-value goods with fewer virgin materials

- In Unilever's and Nike's open-source sharing of process knowledge that saves resources while improving living conditions in emerging nations

- In Nucor's reach for higher levels of industrial ecology in steelmaking through the innovative insights of frontline workers

- In Westpac's awareness that, as a prominent financial intermediary, it has a responsibility to the larger biological and social commons of which it is a part

The energy and insights of all seven Focus Group companies emerge from their life-mimicking fractal structures. Developed from the inside out, these begin with the ways companies inspire employees to engage the powerful neural networks that link their hearts and brains to their biophilic gut instincts. These inner networks, in turn, activate interpersonal networks that reach from small work teams into larger corporate networks of shared purpose and ultimately into the open-source world of knowledge that sustains all forms of evolutionary progress (natural and scientific).

Resistance to renaissance thinking

In spite of evidence supporting the effectiveness of the emerging ecocentric model, most political, economic, and business leaders remain committed to the old industrial capitalist paradigm. As in Renaissance Europe, where kings, lords, and clergy jealously guarded their privileges and hierarchical beliefs, the old guard today fiercely resists the diffusion of authority and power advanced by the new thinking. We see this resistance today in many forms, some of them aggressively defensive (corporate lobbying), some crude (crony capitalism), and some subtle (the meanings people attach to words).

Take the word "economic," for example. To many in the banking industry, flooding markets with cheap credit is economic—in spite of the fact that it disrupts normal price discovery processes and, in so doing, contributes to self-destructive misallocations of resources. (Such practices have led to the acceleration of global debt/GDP ratios since the late 1970s and the increasing volatility of financial markets since the early 1990s, which led to the financial crash of 2008.)

The question of what is economic or uneconomic, in the end, boils down to accounting conventions: whether we take a narrow, linear approach that favors a particular interest group or whether we take a more holistic, full-cost accounting approach that looks to the wellbeing of our shared ecological, economic, and social commons.

The same standard applies to the way we measure GDP, a metric that even its originator (Simon Kuznets) saw as deficient. Conventional theory holds that remedial costs associated with systemic degradation—war, hurricane damage, oil spills, public health epidemics, air and water pollution, etc.—add to GDP although, in reality, these events diminish our collective wellbeing.

By looking only at direct monetary costs and ignoring external costs borne by society and Nature, conventional accounting practices perpetuate the traditional model of industrial capitalism and corporate governance that causes systemic degradation in the first place. Beyond being one-sided, such framing also desensitizes us to the damages we do to the natural world and to each other.

This refusal of the economic establishment to face inconvenient truths is substantiated by Journal-Ranking.com, which ranks 100 economic journals based on the influence of their papers. According to its 2014 rankings, the *Journal of Environmental Economics and Management* ranked 63rd and *Ecological Economics* ranked 100th—far behind *Econometrica,* which ranked third, plus other journals that specialize in quantitative economics.[7] (Just as scholasticism was used to meticulously defend Church dogma during the European Renaissance, the defenders of today's economic orthodoxy cloak their theories in complex equations that give them a veneer of meticulous respectability.)

Based on these rankings, it is not surprising that environmental economists and advocates of full-cost accounting continue to be excluded from the highest levels of government, industry, and university faculties.

The failure of conventional economic theory to see systems as a whole is compounded by the value at risk models of the world's biggest banks, which supply much of the capital used in generating GDP.

When value at risk equations egregiously failed, as they did during the global financial crash of 2008, advocates of the old orthodoxy deflected public attention from the real issue at hand rather than admit these mathematical models were at fault. Instead of framing the crash as the symptom of a larger ecological and social problem of living beyond our means, they framed it as a liquidity problem that could be remediated by infusing public money into the commercial banking system and by lowering to nearly zero the rate commercial banks pay to borrow money from their central

7   Retrieved from http://www.scimagojr.com/journalrank.php?category=0 &area=2000&year=2014&country=&order=sjr&min=0&min_type=cd &page=1.

bank. Thus, the linked problems of ecological overstep, inefficient (linear) accounting procedures, and rising debt ratios were swept under the rug while the costs of humanity's careless overindulgence continued to spin higher as they have from cycle to cycle since the late 1970s.

Thinking beyond GDP and the bottom line

We learn a lot about national economies and companies by what they choose to measure, because metrics ultimately reflect values and goals. Because GDP and other linear accounting methods perpetuate a failed and corrupt system of economic and business management, progressive countries and companies have begun to create more holistic accounting systems.

Canada and Finland, for example, have begun to explore a new metric called the Genuine Progress Indicator (GPI), which assesses environmental and social factors that are not included in GDP. Using a dashboard of 26 indicators, GPI gives a composite picture of gains and losses to the health of the commons in which we all live. These include the costs of social and ecological degradation (such as poverty, environmental remediation, global climate change, and damaged ecosystems), plus uncompensated value added (self-education, volunteer work) that are not currently incorporated in GDP.

By accounting for the substantial externalized costs borne by society as a whole, GPI gives a more balanced picture of real economic progress. Although approximate and still evolving, these metrics put us on a more sustainable path than the purported mathematical precision of GDP. (As systems thinkers are fond of saying, it is better to be generally right than precisely wrong.)

According to one GPI calculation, the net economic growth of the U.S.A. has been stagnant since the 1970s[8]—a finding that roughly correlates with the decline of the American middle class and the time when humanity's ecological footprint began to exceed the Earth's biological carrying capacity.

Orthodox economists, of course, object to GPI, saying it is vulnerable to political manipulation. But one can say the same for GDP. According to *The Atlantic*, corporations now spend $2.6 billion a year on lobbying.[9] That works out to nearly $4.9 million per member of Congress.

In weighing which is the better metric, or if there is another better metric, the question ultimately becomes: what values do we most care to use in measuring progress? Also, how do we define progress? Is it purely economic? Related to human wellbeing? More pointedly, is it wise to ignore statistical evidence that world economic growth is today using up the resources of more than 1.6 planet Earths? Or that the world's supplies of fresh water are being used up and polluted faster than they can be replenished?

Progressive companies wrestle with the same issues. For this reason, companies that mimic life develop balanced scorecard metrics that look beyond sales and earnings to their ecological impacts, employee health, and other forward-looking indicators of relational equity. When they disclose such information on corporate websites and in annual reports, they invite stakeholder feedback, which accelerates their capacities to learn and deliver appropriate service. Full disclosure also builds public trust, which generates

8   Redefining Progress (n.d.). Genuine Progress Indicator. Retrieved from http://rprogress.org/sustainability_indicators/genuine_progress_indicator.htm.

9   Lee Drutman (2015, April 20). How corporate lobbyists conquered American democracy. *The Atlantic.* Retrieved from http://www.theatlantic.com/business/archive/2015/04/how-corporate-lobbyists-conquered-american-democracy/390822/.

customer and shareholder loyalty. Taken together, these feed the overlapping cycles shown in Figure 9.1 that support company sales and profits.

Unilever is a good example of this more integrated approach to reporting. As noted in Chapter 1, the company is committed to halving by 2020 the environmental footprint associated with the production and use of its products relative to 2010. In keeping with its intent to maintain a broad systems view, its strategic plan contains nine medium-term commitments concerning its social, environmental, and economic performance, plus specific short-term goals that will help it achieve its objectives. Metrics include a variety of gauges, such as environmental and occupational safety indicators, and specific targets intended to measure progress, including greenhouse gas emissions, water use, the nutritional value of products, opportunities for women, postconsumer waste, and sustainable sourcing.

To the Harvard Business School professor, Robert G. Eccles, such integrated reporting (IR) is a higher form of sustainability reporting: a self-reinforcing cycle that will result in more "efficient and productive capital allocation." By reporting cultural values and sustainability metrics alongside business results and financial metrics, it enables stakeholders to see the correlations between these activities. In doing so, it performs a "transformation" function, encouraging deeper commitments to ecocentric management practices.[10]

Like GPI reporting, which looks to the economic, ecological, and social health of the commons in which we live, IR remains a relatively new and underutilized tool. Of the seven companies profiled in this book, six—Novo Nordisk, Henkel, Nike, Unilever, United Technologies, and Westpac—currently use some form of IR. Given

10 See IIRC (2013). *The International <IR> Framework*. Retrieved from http://integratedreporting.org/wp-content/uploads/2013/12/13-12-08-THE-INTERNATIONAL-IR-FRAMEWORK-2-1.pdf.

the early stage of IR development—framework guidelines on reporting principles were first introduced in 2013—this high participation rate is exceptional.

Although less detailed in its reporting on sustainability matters, the seventh of our companies, Nucor, does provide on its website easy-to-access current information on its workplace safety, environmental footprint, community outreach, and financial results. And it is clear in reporting these results that its corporate culture and sense of responsibility are what makes it the world's most productive steel company.

> An integrated report is a concise communication about how an organization's strategy, governance, performance and prospects, in the context of its external environment, lead to the creation of value in the short, medium and long term.
>
> International Integrated Reporting Council (IIRC)[11]

When it comes to the content of reporting, Eccles and Harvard colleague George Serafeim say:

> There is no clear way to measure the number of companies that are issuing integrated reports. Rather the practice of integrated reporting is a matter of degree. There are companies that are doing more or less integrated reporting and firms that practice to a certain extent integrated reporting while not describing their reports as integrated.[12]

---

11   IIRC (n.d.). Integrated Reporting (IR). Retrieved from http://integrated reporting.org.

12   Robert G. Eccles & George Serafeim (2014). Corporate and integrated reporting: a functional perspective, p. 8. Retrieved from http://ssrn.com/ abstract=2388716.

The important thing about GPI and IR as new reporting methods is their capacity to see systems as a whole, to define progress in regenerative new ways. As such, they open our minds to the health of the living commons in which all commerce operates and thereby enable us to see the connections between systemic health and economic results. In doing so they challenge the old order—just as humanism, the rule of law, and freedom of religion challenged the rule of kings and popes during the European Renaissance.

In both of these evolutionary periods, we see power diffused from entrenched hierarchies and spread to empowered individuals as people search for new insights into the way the world works. This was one of Ken Iverson's key insights when he transformed Nucor in 1965 into an employee-centered company and it is why Nucor today remains the technology and sustainability leader of its industry with no R&D department.

Toward Nature as a model

Companies that mimic life use Nature as a model because it is the most resilient and self-energizing system we know. With its exceptionally diverse and diffuse base of knowledge, Nature has survived, evolved, and thrived over billions of years.

By adopting this standard, ecocentric models go beyond challenging corporate and political hierarchies. They challenge the very notion that humanity has a divine right—as Descartes and Bacon supposed—to be "masters and possessors of Nature."

Living assets (people and Nature) cannot be mastered and possessed in the same way as nonliving (capital) assets, because they have, at a minimum, the qualities of self-possession and self-making that transcend inert things. To achieve their full potential, we must respect and nurture their inherent capacities to self-organize, learn, and adapt.

To many business owners and managers, property rights include the right to debilitate (and even destroy) what they own. While this is usually protected under the law, at least as it pertains to land and capital equipment, it is ultimately self-destructive. Once an asset is harmed, it loses its future productive potential both to the current owner and to the ecological commons of which it is a part.

But the harm doesn't stop there. It can be, and often is, infectious. Think of a river system, where upstream property owners deprive downstream people of access to clean water, or an oil refinery that sickens people with its airborne emissions. In both cases the owners believe they are acting within their rights, but in doing so they harm the commons. When the costs of maintaining the commons approach or surpass the benefits the commons once offered, that property becomes an ecological and economic liability. Everyone is worse off. Social and economic cohesion breaks down.

Kalundborg succeeds as a model community because it respects life within the commons. Starting in the 1960s, it organized around water savings to protect a local aquifer and today recycles 3 million m³ of water for the benefit of nearby companies, farms, and residents. Today, as a highly evolved circular economy, nearby residents, businesses, and the environment all prosper.

Stewardship is inherent in Nature via self-regenerating processes that have evolved over billions of years. As a human ethic, it embodies responsible care rather than pushing ownership rights to the point of harming the commons. In corporate management, that means treating all life with respect and helping employees grow to their fullest potential.

The wonderful thing about stewardship is the positive energy it generates wherever it comes into play. As described in the previous chapters, the deeper companies go into LAS, the healthier they and the commons become. And the greater their shareholder returns.

By this standard, LAS is a dynamic win–win proposition. As an antidote to the downward spiral of industrial capitalism, it opens a new age of human development and harmony with Nature. The catalyst for this resides in the complex neurology of our hearts and brains and the biophilic wiring of our gut instincts, which we are just getting to know and understand.

Epilogue

> Life is sacred, that is to say, it is the supreme
> value, to which all other values are subordinate.
>
> Albert Einstein

There is nothing wrong with capitalism itself. Its capacity to generate ideas, raise capital, and adapt to changing circumstances surpasses all human institutions. But there is something very wrong with a system that puts profit ahead of life—as industrial capitalism does—because life is the very source of profit.

What is needed, then, is a compelling new theory of capitalism—one that recognizes and builds on this obvious fact. That is what living asset stewardship (LAS) does. Based on results of the Global LAMP Index® over more than two decades, the effectiveness of LAS, measured in financial, ecological, and social terms, far surpasses the older system of industrial capitalism.

This is not to say that LAS, as practiced by our seven Focus Group companies, is perfect. In spite of their demonstrated successes, they still have a long way to go before they live and work within the limits of the Earth's biological resources. This is due in part to the fact that ecocentric management theory is still relatively new. It is also due to the inertia of old habits (for example, our preference for quick solutions, which often leads us to treat symptoms rather than causes).

In addition, when the world is perceived in terms of oversimplified metrics, such as GDP or market performance, we fail to recognize that it is actually a web of interdependent, overlapping networks (ecosystems, social systems, economic systems) where the health and wellbeing of individual parts are ultimately dependent on the health of the whole.

To get to that next level of awareness—where we see our economic lives in terms of the larger web of life—we must let go of our egos and allow our spiritual intelligence, which is more in tune with the natural world, to assert itself. Framed in terms of our natural instincts, this fuses our genetic love of life with our instinctual desire to survive.

As illustrated by our seven Focus Group exemplars, the deeper we dive in this direction (the deeper we go into LAS), the more leverage we achieve in attaining the positive ecological, social, and economic results we want.

When discussing models of corporate stewardship, people often ask why some firms that pursue triple bottom line agendas fail to achieve the performance results of LAMP companies. The overwhelming reason is that they are trapped in the industrial capitalist mind-set of hierarchical command-and-control, and in the belief that the firm is above the living world in which it exists. The core problem here is that a mechanistic management system cannot be bolted on to an ecocentric set of values. The two systems clash.

For companies to truly excel, they must step away from the old mechanistic paradigm—as Nucor did in 1965 and as Nike did in the early 1990s—and reinvent themselves from the inside out.

Commenting on the operating leverage of such paradigmatic changes, the renowned systems thinker Donella Meadows said:

"Leverage points are places within a complex system (a corporation, an economy, a living body, a city, an ecosystem) where a small shift in one thing can produce big changes in everything."[1]

From this perspective, the ecocentric model of LAS is a key leverage point. Once companies fully adopt it in place of the old industrial capitalist model, everything indeed changes. The key insight in this paradigmatic shift is that economic, corporate, and financial systems are, in reality, subsystems of Nature and function best when they function as natural systems.

Sadly, proponents of the old paradigm don't get this. In fact, as their business systems break down, they do the opposite. By borrowing more and more to prop up a self-destructing system, they make everything worse: from climate change and ecosystem destruction to economic and financial risk.

On top of all this, the world today is enmeshed in continuous warfare as world population growth collides with an ecologically degraded and corrupted commons. Although most intense in the impoverished regions of South-East Asia, the Middle East, and the Sahel region of central Africa, no region is safe from conflict, including the U.S.A., Europe, Russia, and China.

In the sweep of history, this situation parallels that of Europe in the century that gave birth to the Renaissance: an era marked by the corrupt regimes of popes and kings, the Hundred Years War (1337–1453), unthinkable cruelty to dissenters, and the filth-borne bubonic plague, which killed a third of Europe's population. To people living in those times, it must have seemed as if everything was falling apart. And yet, like today, the chaos was not an ending, but a beginning.

---

1   Donella Meadows (1999). Leverage points: places to intervene in a system. Retrieved from http://donellameadows.org/archives/leverage-points-places-to-intervene-in-a-system/.

End of the beginning

Climate change and ecosystem destruction, like the plague, is a harsh wake-up call that has catalyzed transformative new thinking. But there's a big difference here. Whereas the plague threatened human life, today's ecological degradation threatens all life.

The fatal flaw of Renaissance humanism was its propensity to become self-centered. Although it liberated Europe from debilitating feudal tyrannies, from the Enlightenment onward it conveyed the erroneous message that humanity was above Nature—entitled to take what we want, when we want, heedless of our impacts on the rest of life.

In our subsequent dash for production and capital growth—supported by Say's Law that production creates its own demand, and seconded by *laissez-faire* economic thinking—we have so compromised the Earth's biological resources that scientists have begun to call the industrial era of the past two centuries the "anthropocene," a name that reflects the ubiquitous, mostly damaging, effects of human activities on all of Earth's systems and processes.

As we awaken to the growing dangers of the anthropocene, we find ourselves looking more deeply into our intimate connections to the rest of life and the need for governance norms that recognize those connections. Companies that mimic life today show how effective those norms can be in a market economy.

Just as Renaissance thinking evolved into laws that protect our individual rights and freedoms, we need new laws today that recognize the sanctity of the biospheric web of life, which underpins those very rights and freedoms.

Such laws need not be burdensome. Simpler is better. Markets respond well to commonsense principles, especially ones that regenerate the biosphere and, in so doing, contribute to the quality of human life.

Increasingly, companies that mimic life support governments in advancing ecocentric laws and regulations by setting standards of what can be done such as those at Kalundborg, by supporting initiatives such as the UN Global Compact, and by actively campaigning for new legislation.

Nike's innovative BICEP (Business for Innovative Climate & Energy Policy) coalition is a cogent example of such proactive behavior. This group of 38 consumer brand companies (year-end 2015 total)—including LAMP exemplars Unilever, L'Oreal, and Nestlé—is committed to advancing "meaningful energy and climate legislation that will enable a rapid transition to a low-carbon, 21st century economy that will create new jobs and stimulate economic growth while stabilizing our planet's fragile climate." Companies wedded to the old industrial capitalist paradigm will certainly resist such change initiatives. However, they must admit that corporate leaders, such as those at Kalundborg and those committed to BICEP, have proven a point: that real corporate responsibility, defined here as LAS, correlates with profitability. More pointedly, as the seven companies profiled in this book illustrate, the deeper they go in this direction, the better their profits and credit ratings are likely to be and the longer they are likely to survive.

It is hard to argue with such outcomes—especially for companies that avow a commitment to "hard" tangible results.

The emergent truth is that LAS is more than a means to improve corporate results. It reflects a giant evolutionary step forward in human consciousness—one that reconnects us to the web of life that is the source of everything we value. At a time of unprecedented ecological, social, and economic stress, it is our bridge to the future.

Appendix 1:
The Global LAMP Index®

Company	Founded	Company	Founded
3M	1902	Iberdrola	1901
Alcoa	1886	IBM	1911
American Express	1860	ING Groep	1845
Amgen	1980	Intel	1968
Applied Materials	1967	Johnson & Johnson	1886
Baxter International	1931	Kyocera	1959
Berkshire Hathaway	1963	L'Oreal	1909
Canon	1933	Marriott International	1927
Cemex	1906	Medtronic	1949
Electrolux	1901	Nestlé	1866
Fedex	1913	Nike	1964
GlaxoSmithKline	1715	Norsk Hydro	1905
Google	1996	Novo Nordisk	1923
Grupo Santander	1857	Nucor	1955
Henkel	1876	Panasonic	1918
Herman Miller	1905	Pearson	1844
Hewlett-Packard	1939	Philips Electronics	1891
Home Depot	1978	Procter & Gamble	1837
HSBC Holdings	1865	Rio Tinto	1873

Company	Founded
Royal Dutch/Shell	1907
SAP	1972
Siemens	1847
Skanska	1887
Southwest Airline	1971
Standard Chartered	1853
Starbucks	1971
Statoil	1972
Stora Enso	1288
Suncor	1917
Swiss Re	1863

Company	Founded
Target	1881
TD Bank	1855
Telefónica	1924
Texas Instruments	1939
Toyota	1937
Unilever	1855
United Technologies	1929
Vodafone	1982
Volvo	1915
Walgreens	1901
Westpac Banking	1817

These 60 companies were selected as best-of-breed exemplars of living asset stewardship (LAS) within a representative sample of industries/sectors that correlate with major global market indices. The original selection process took place mainly between 1995 and 2003.

History of the index

The first iteration of the index was in 1995, at which time it numbered only 50 companies. All seven of the companies profiled in this book were in that original cohort.

Between 1996 and 2004 the original index was expanded to 60 companies in order to make it more representative of the industry/sector diversity of its primary comparators: the MSCI World Index, the FTSE World Index, the S&P Global 100, and the S&P 500 Index.

During this period, as the definition of LAS evolved, some names were dropped from the original LAMP50 and others added. In 2004 the Index was finalized as a learning lab and resource for my book, *Profit For Life* (Cambridge, MA: Society for Organizational Learning, 2006).

Since 2006 there have been six name changes in the index: two were due to acquisitions (Iberdrola's of Scottish Power; Santander's of ABN AMRO); one was due to Microsoft's acquisition of Nokia's handset business, at which time we replaced Nokia with Google; and three were replacements necessitated by initial selection errors on my part. In each case when a substitution was made, I entered the new company in the index on the appropriate swap date. This was also the standard used when Northfield Information Services calculated the performance data revealed in Appendix 2.

All companies selected for the Global LAMP Index® have been observed through a minimum of two economic cycles. This practice screens out fair-weather stewards (companies that abandon their stewardship principles during cyclical downturns).

Standing the test of time

The average age of companies in the Global LAMP Index® exceeds 117 years and the median exceeds a century. By contrast, the average tenure of an S&P 500 firm has shrunk to 18 years.[1] And it is declining.

So what is it about life-mimicking companies that gives them this longevity? It apparently starts with a cultural respect for life and a desire to make a difference in the world.

---

1   Innosight (2012). *Creative Destruction Whips Through North America*, p. 2. Retrieved from http://www.innosight.com/innovation-resources/strategy-innovation/upload/creative-destruction-whips-through-corporate-america_final2015.pdf.

Arie de Geus, in his 1997 classic, "The living company," puts it
this way:

> What I have come to call *living companies* have a personality
> that allows them to evolve harmoniously. They know who they
> are, understand how they fit into the world, value new ideas
> and new people, and husband their money in a way that allows
> them to govern their future.[2]

In broad terms, that is a good general description of companies
that mimic life. But there is more to their staying power as we have
discovered in this book.

While one may agree or disagree that the companies in the index
today belong in our select group of LAS exemplars, those that have
survived for a century or more have done a remarkable job of learning and adapting as the world about them changes.

---

2   Arie de Geus (1997). The living company. *Harvard Business Review*, March–
April. Retrieved from https://hbr.org/1997/03/the-living-company.

Appendix 2:
Global LAMP Index® returns vs. comparator indices

Year	Global Lamp Index®			Global comparator indices		
	Focus Group	Equal weight	Mkt cap weight	FTSE World	MSCI World	S&P Glob 100
1995	40.05	37.63	32.46	19.61	21.32	40.09
1996	37.53	29.22	30.30	13.21	14.00	25.54
1997	20.21	32.61	27.01	15.40	16.23	30.01
1998	16.60	30.07	32.37	23.03	24.80	33.21
1999	2.60	41.91	36.35	26.00	25.34	32.79
2000	11.17	4.23	-8.74	-11.08	-12.92	-12.56
2001	2.15	-3.41	-9.52	-16.15	-16.52	-13.81
2002	-5.73	-12.20	-19.13	-19.06	-19.54	-22.59
2003	41.96	43.21	34.92	33.91	33.76	26.25
2004	31.96	17.74	10.59	16.05	15.25	6.43
2005	11.48	12.26	7.31	11.32	10.02	1.17
2006	35.56	23.60	19.01	21.47	20.65	18.47
2007	31.02	11.64	14.11	11.32	9.57	6.12

Year	Global Lamp Index®			Global comparator indices		
	Focus Group	Equal weight	Mkt cap weight	FTSE World	MSCI World	S&P Glob 100
2008	-30.93	-39.35	-36.69	-40.91	-40.33	-35.31
2009	42.37	52.39	35.81	34.38	30.79	22.29
2010	20.93	13.91	6.85	12.73	12.34	12.51
2011	1.97	-8.28	-2.31	-6.48	-5.02	3.18
2012	25.58	18.53	14.32	16.96	16.54	16.05
2013	29.06	31.44	27.49	24.68	27.37	30.09
2014	4.26	8.48	5.51	4.77	5.50	12.74
2015	6.81	-5.70	-2.71	2.58	-1.84	2.63
Avg	18.69	16.19	12.16	9.23	8.55	11.22

Compound annual growth

Year	Global Lamp Index®			Global comparator indices		
	Focus group	Equal weight	Mkt cap weight	FTSE World	MSCI World	S&P Glob 100
All yrs	2407.12	1446.75	671.36	348.63	326.55	546.91
20 yrs	1618.76	1023.85	482.33	275.09	251.59	361.78
15 yrs	781.70	240.89	133.63	108.29	94.80	82.92
10 yrs	288.71	112.36	82.35	77.41	71.00	101.68
5 yrs	84.04	46.18	46.15	46.57	47.54	80.23
3 yrs	43.72	34.46	30.87	34.00	31.92	50.52
1 yr	6.81	-5.70	-2.71	2.58	-1.84	2.63

Sources:
Northfield Information Services (http://www.northinfo.com) for Global LAMP Index®
Financial Times Stock Exchange indices (www.ftserussell.com)
Morgan Stanley Capital indices (https://www.msci.com)

Appendix 3: Moody's credit ratings on LAMP companies

Company	Long-term unsecured debt		Short-term debt rating	Notes
	2015 rating	10-year range		
3M	Aa3	Aa1 to Aa3	Prime-1	
Alcoa	Ba1	A2 to Ba1	SGL1	Outlook positive
American Express	A3	A1 to A3	Prime-2	
Amgen	Baa1	A2 to Baa1	Prime-2	
Applied Materials	A3	Consistent A3	Prime-2	
Baxter International	Baa2	Baa2 to A3	Prime-2	
Berkshire Hathaway	Aa2	Aaa to Aa2	Prime-1	
Canon	Aa1	Aa3 to Aa1	NR	
Cemex	NR	Ba1 to Baa3	NR	S&P B+ (stable)
Electrolux	NR	Baa1 to Baa2	NR	S&P BBB (stable)
Fedex	Baa1	Baa2 to Baa1	Prime-2	

Company	Long-term unsecured debt		Short-term debt rating	Notes
	2015 rating	10-year range		
GlaxoSmith Kline	A2	Aa2 to A2	Prime-1	
Google	Aa2	NR to Aa2	Prime-1	
Grupo Santander	A3	A1 to Baa1	Prime-2	
Henkel	A2	A1 to A2	Prime-1	
Herman Miller	NR	Baa2 to Baa3	NR	S&P BBB
Hewlett-Packard	Baa2	A3 to Baa2	Prime-2	
Home Depot	A2	Aa3 to A2	Prime-1	
HSBC Holdings	Aa2	Aa2 to Aa3	Prime-1	
Iberdrola	Baa1	A2 to Baa1	Prime-2	
IBM	Aa3	A1 to Aa3	Prime-1	
ING Groep	A1	Aa2 to A3	Prime-1	
Intel	A1	A2 to A1	Prime-1	
Johnson & Johnson	Aaa	Consistent Aaa	Prime-1	
Kyocera	NR	A1 to Aa3	NR	Cash > debt
L'Oreal	NR	No ratings	Prime-1	Cash > debt
Marriott International	Baa2	Baa3 to Baa2	Prime-2	
Medtronic	A3	A1 to A3	Prime-2	
Nestlé	Aa2	Aaa to Aa2	Prime-1	
Nike	A1	A2 to A1	Prime-1	
Norsk Hydro	Baa2	A1 to Baa2	NR	
Novo Nordisk	A1	A2 to A1	Prime-1	
Nucor	Baa1	A1 to Baa1	Prime-2	
Panasonic	Baa1	Aa3 to Baa2	NR	
Pearson	Baa1	Consistent Baa1	NR	
Philips Electronics	Baa1	A3 to Baa1	Prime-2	

Company	Long-term unsecured debt		Short-term debt rating	Notes
	2015 rating	10-year range		
Procter & Gamble	Aa3	Consistent Aa3	Prime-1	
Rio Tinto	A3	Aa3 to A3	NR	
Royal Dutch/ Shell	Aa1	Consistent Aa1	Prime-1	
SAP	A2	NR to A2	Prime-1	
Siemens	A1	A1 to Aa3	Prime-1	
Skanska	NR	No Ratings	NR	Cash > debt
Southwest Airline	Baa1	Baa2 to Baa1	NR	
Standard Chartered	Aa2	A2 to Aa2	Prime-1	
Starbucks	A2	Baa2 to A2	Prime-1	
Statoil	Aa2	NR to Aa2	Prime-1	
Stora Enso	Ba2	Baa2 to Ba2	NR	
Suncor	Baa1	Baa2 to A3	Prime-2	
Swiss Re	Aa3	Aa1 to Aa3	Prime-1	
Target	A2	Consistent A2	Prime-1	
TD Bank	Aa1	Aa3 to Aa1	Prime-1	
Telefónica	Baa2	A3 to Baa2	Prime-2	
Texas Instruments	A1	A2 to A1	Prime-1	
Toyota	Aa3	Aaa to Aa3	Prime-1	
Unilever	A1	Consistent A1	Prime-1	
United Technologies	A3	A2 to A3	Prime-2	
Vodafone	Baa1	A2 to Baa1	Prime-2	
Volvo	Baa2	A3 to Baa2	Prime-2	
Walgreens	Baa2	Aa3 to Baa2	Prime-2	
Westpac Banking	Aa2	Aa1 to Aa2	Prime-1	

Investment grade ratings	# of LAMP companies	% of LAMP companies	
Aa3 and higher	14	23.33	
A3 to A1	19	31.66	
Baa3 to Baa1	15	25.00	
Total investment grade	**48**	**80.00**	**Median rating A3**
Non-rated (NR) companies with low net debt/equity	5	8.33	

Notes:

1. Not all creditworthy companies seek ratings. Among those rated NR, three regularly have more cash than debt (Kyocera, L'Oreal, Skanska) and two (Electrolux, Herman Miller) have moderate net debt/equity ratios.

2. Alcoa's rating (Ba1) reflects mainly the cyclicality of its industry.

3. Cemex (NR) is close to having its investment grade rating restored.

4. Stora Enso (Ba2), which was founded in 1288, is one of the world's oldest companies. Its net debt/equity ratio is a moderate 53%.

About the author

Joseph (Jay) Bragdon is a money manager for high net worth families and a
pioneer in the field of corporate stewardship. In 1972 he published the first
empirical work linking stewardship to
profitability (titled "Is Pollution Profitable?") and cochaired the first U.S.
symposium on "Corporate Responsi-
bility in Investments" at the Harvard Business School. From that
time on, he has tracked the evolution of stewardship best practices
and their impacts on corporate profitability.

As that evolution progressed, he began to see it as a renaissance
in corporate thinking where leadership companies, discerning the
anomalies of industrial capitalism, began to model themselves as
living systems. In doing so they placed a higher value on living
assets (people and Nature) than on nonliving capital assets—in
effect reversing norms that had arisen from the Industrial Revolution.

To test the validity of this observation, in the mid-1990s Jay created a learning lab of companies that were exemplars in their care
of living assets—a practice he called "living asset stewardship"

(LAS). The lab, which is named the Global Living Asset Management Performance (LAMP) Index®, focuses on 60 companies that were at the time of their selection best-of-breed LAS practitioners in diverse industries/sectors.

Noting how LAS and profitability reinforced one another over time through a process of continuous learning, Jay wrote *Profit For Life*, which was published in 2006 by the Society for Organizational Learning.

Companies That Mimic Life conveys his most recent research on stewardship best practices. As a window on the new renaissance thinking, it affirms that the deeper companies go into LAS, the more profitable they become.

Jay is married to Jeanne Veatch Bragdon (pictured left). Both are former colleagues of the late Donella Meadows—to whom this book is dedicated—and have served on the board of the institute she founded.

Printed in the United States
by Baker & Taylor Publisher Services